Chocolate & Baking

p

This is a Parragon Publishing Book
This edition published in 2002

Parragon Publishing
Queen Street House
4 Queen Street
Bath BA1 1HE, UK

Copyright © Parragon 2000

ISBN: 0-75257-558-9

A copy of the CIP data for this book is available from the British
Library, upon request.

Printed in China

Note

Cup measurements used in this book are for American cups.
Tablespoons are assumed to be 15 ml. Unless otherwise stated,
milk is assumed to be full fat, eggs are medium, and pepper is
freshly ground black pepper.

Contents

Introduction

Chocolate is one of life's luxuries and one of the few that we can all afford. This book contains all of the recipes you need to enjoy this luxury at any time of the day. For example, you could wake up to Pain au Chocolat, or have a tasty chocolate cookie with morning coffee. You could indulge in a hot chocolate pudding at lunch time, have a sumptuous slice of chocolate cake with afternoon tea, luxuriate with a rich chocolate dessert as part of an evening meal, and round off the end of the day with a hot chocolate toddy. Whilst this might seem to be taking things too far, even for the most hardened chocoholic, why not tempt yourself with a perfect chocolate treat now and then. Go on, spoil yourself!

Chocolate is produced from the beans of the cacao tree, which originated in South America, and now grows in Africa, the West Indies, the tropical parts of America, and the Far East. Cacao beans are large pods—once harvested, both the pulp from the pods and the bean are allowed to ferment in the sun. The pulp evaporates and the bean develops its chocolatey flavor. The outer skin is then removed and the beans are left in the sun for a little longer or roasted. Finally, they are shelled and the kernels are used for making cocoa and chocolate.

The kernels have to be ground and processed to produce a thick mixture or paste called "cocoa solids", and it is this that we refer to when gauging the quality of chocolate. The cocoa solids are then pressed to remove some of the fat—"cocoa butter." They are then further processed to produce the product that we know and love as chocolate.

STORING CHOCOLATE

Store chocolate in a cool, dry place away from direct heat or sunlight. Most chocolate can be stored for about one year. It can be stored in the refrigerator, but make sure it is well wrapped as it will pick up flavors from other foods. Chocolate decorations can be stored in airtight containers and interleaved with non-stick baking parchment. Dark chocolate will keep for four weeks and milk and white chocolate for two weeks.

MELTING CHOCOLATE

Chocolate should not be melted over direct heat, except when melted with other ingredients, and even then the heat should be very low.

Break the chocolate into small, equal-sized pieces and place them in a heatproof bowl. Place over a pan of hot water, making sure the base is not in contact with the water. Once the chocolate starts to melt, stir gently and if necessary leave over the water a little longer. No drops of water or steam should come into contact with the melted chocolate as it will solidify.

To melt chocolate in the microwave, break it into small pieces and place in microwave-proof bowl. Timing will vary according to the type and quantity of chocolate. As a guide, melt $4\frac{1}{2}$ ounces dark chocolate on High for two-three minutes on Medium. Stir the chocolate and leave to stand for a few minutes, then stir again. Return the chocolate to the microwave for a further 30 seconds if necessary.

SETTING CHOCOLATE

Chocolate sets best at 65°F although it will set (more slowly) in a slightly hotter room. If possible, set chocolate for decorations in a cool room. If set in the refrigerator, it may develop a white bloom.

TYPES OF CHOCOLATE

Dark Chocolate *can contain anything from 30% to 75% cocoa solids. It has a slightly sweet flavor and a dark color. It is the chocolate most used in cooking. For everyday cooking and the majority of the recipes for dark chocolate, choose one with around 50% cocoa solids. However, dark chocolate with a higher cocoa solid content will give a richer, more intense, flavor. This chocolate is often called luxury or continental chocolate and has a cocoa solid content of between 70-75%. Occasionally it is essential to use a better chocolate and I have indicated in the individual recipes where this is the case.*

Milk Chocolate, *as its name suggests, contains milk and has a lovely creamy, mild, and sweet flavor. It is mostly used as an eating chocolate, rather than in cooking. However, it does have its place in chocolate cookery, especially for decorations, and when a milder, creamy flavor is required. It is more sensitive to heat than dark chocolate so care must be taken when melting it.*

White Chocolate
contains a lower cocoa butter content and cocoa solids. It can be quite temperamental when used in cooking. Always choose a luxury white cooking chocolate to avoid problems and take great care not to overheat when melting. White chocolate is useful for color contrast, especially when decorating cakes.

Couverture *is the preferred chocolate for professionals (it retains a high gloss after melting and cooling) but it requires tempering and is only available from specialist suppliers and has therefore not been used in this book.*

Chocolate-Flavored Cake Covering *is an inferior product not generally used by true chocolate lovers. However, it has a high fat content, making it easier to handle when making some decorations such as curls or caraque. If you do not want to compromise the flavor too much, but have difficulty making the decorations with pure chocolate, try adding a few squares of chocolate-flavored cake covering to a good quality chocolate.*

Chocolate Chips
are available in dark, milk, and white chocolate varieties, and are used for baking and decoration.

Coco Powder *is the powder left after the cocoa butter has been pressed from the roasted and ground beans. It is unsweetened and bitter in flavor. It gives a good, strong chocolate flavor when used in cooking.*

In addition to the chocolate recipes, this book brings you all the skills you need to recreate some of the best-loved traditional baking dishes. It also shows you how to experiment with some exciting contemporary ingredients now readily available in leading supermarkets.

Clear step-by-step instructions guide you through the techniques needed to mastermind all the baking favorites that have been savored and enjoyed from generation to generation.

FAMILY FAVORITES

Experience the sweet pleasure of a wonderful selection of everyday and special occasion desserts as you learn how to make rich, gooey, and irresistible puddings such Pavlova, Fruit Crumble, Queen of Puddings, and tasty sticky chocolate puddings. Everyone's favorite is sure to be included.

This book also helps you to perfect your baking skills so that you are guaranteed to have success every single time you prepare a dish, whether it be an elaborate cheesecake, a chocolate feast, or a fruity crumble.

BREADS & SAVORIES

Making bread at home is great fun and allows you to experiment with all sorts of ingredients, such as sun-dried tomatoes, garlic, mangoes, and olive oil, to create versatile and delicious variations of modern breads. Easy-blend yeast makes the task of bread-making less time-consuming these days. Chapter 4 also shows you how to spice-up all sorts of savories with exciting adaptations of traditional flans, pies, and, scones.

VEGETARIAN COOKING

Vegetarian recipes full of delicious wholesome ingredients, which are every bit as good as traditional baking favorites, have been created for those following a vegetarian diet.

CAKES & COOKIES

Transform traditional cakes and cookies into a real tea-time extravaganza with some new adaptations of old favorites.

Irresistible cake recipes are included, as are delicious cookie recipes. These recipes are quick and easy to make, and are sure to be winners with all of the family.

PUDDINGS

Puddings are always a great treat at the end of a meal, but they must be balanced with the rest of the food. Rich puddings after a heavy main course will not be popular. This book provides myriad ideas, both light and more substantial, to round of a meal in a perfect manner. Ice cream may be the perfect choice following a heavy roast, while a tasty tart complements a fish main course perfectly.

MAKING CAKES

With all baking recipes, there are some basic principles that apply, and this is especially true of cake making:

- Start by reading the recipe all the way through.
- Weigh all the ingredients accurately and do basic preparation, such as grating and chopping, before you start cooking.
- Basic cake-making ingredients should be kept at room temperature.
- Mixtures that are creamed together, a process which involves mixing butter and sugar together, should be almost white and have a "soft dropping" consistency. This can be done by hand, but using a hand-held electric mixer will save you time and effort.
- "Folding in" is achieved by using a metal spoon or spatula, and working as gently as possible to fold through the flour or dry ingredients in a figure-of-eight movement.
- Do not remove a cake from the oven until it is fully cooked. To test if a cake is cooked, press the surface lightly with your fingertips—it should feel springy to the touch. Alternatively, insert a fine metal skewer into the center of the cake —it will come out clean if the cake is cooked through.
- Leave cakes in their pans to cool before carefully turning out on to a wire rack to cool completely.

MAKING PIES & TARTS

When making the pies or tarts in the book, follow these basic principles:

- Strain the dry ingredients into a large mixing bowl, add the diced fat, and toss it through the flour.
- Gently rub the fat between your fingertips, a little at a time, until the mixture looks like fine breadcrumbs and, as you rub in the mixture, lift your hands up to aerate the mixture as it falls back into the bowl.
- Bind the mixture with iced water or other liquid, using just enough to make a soft dough. Wrap the dough and leave to chill for at least 30 minutes.

Cakes & Gateaux

It is hard to resist the pleasure of a sumptuous
piece of chocolate cake and no baking book would
be complete without a selection of family cakes and
gateaux—there are plenty to choose from in this
chapter. You can spend several indulgent hours in
the kitchen making that perfect extravagant gateau
or to knock up a quick cake for afternoon tea; the
choice is yours. The more experimental among you
can vary the fillings or decorations used according to
what takes your fancy.

Alternatively, follow our easy step-by-step
instructions and look at our pictures to guide
you to perfect results. The gateaux in this book will
be perfectly at home on the dessert table—they are a
feast for the eyes and will keep all hardened cake
addicts in ecstasy. The recipes are ideal for those
who find a slice of cake comforting at any time
of day, as many of them are made with
surprising ease.

Chocolate Almond Cake

Serves 8–10

INGREDIENTS

6 ounces dark chocolate
^{3}/4 cup butter
^{2}/3 cup superfine sugar
4 eggs, separated
^{1}/4 tsp cream of tartar
^{1}/3 cup self-rising flour

1^1/4 cups ground almonds
1 tsp almond extract

TOPPING:
4^1/2 ounces milk chocolate
2 tbsp butter

4 tbsp heavy cream

TO DECORATE:
2 tbsp toasted slivered almonds
1 ounce dark chocolate, melted

1 Lightly grease and flour the base of a 9-inch round springform pan. Break the chocolate into small pieces and place in a small pan with the butter. Heat gently, stirring until melted and well combined.

2 Place 7 tbsp of the superfine sugar in a bowl with the egg yolks and beat until the mixture is pale and creamy. Add the melted chocolate mixture, beating until well combined.

3 Sift the cream of tartar and flour together and fold into the chocolate mixture, together with the ground almonds and almond extract.

4 Beat the egg whites in a bowl until standing in soft peaks. Add the remaining superfine sugar and beat for about 2 minutes by hand, or 45–60 seconds if using an electric mixer, until thick and glossy. Carefully fold the egg whites into the chocolate mixture and spoon into the pan.

Bake in a preheated oven at 375°F for 40 minutes, until just springy to the touch. Let cool.

5 Heat the topping ingredients in a double boiler. Remove from the heat and beat for 2 minutes. Chill in the refrigerator for 30 minutes. Transfer the cake to a plate and spread with the topping. Scatter with the almonds and drizzle with melted chocolate. Allow to set for 2 hours before serving.

Chocolate Tray Bake

Serves 15

INGREDIENTS

1 cup superfine sugar

1 cup soft margarine

4 eggs, beaten

4 tbsp milk

3 cups self-rising flour, sifted

3 tbsp cocoa powder, sifted

$^1/_3$ cup milk chocolate chips

$^1/_3$ cup dark chocolate chips

$^1/_3$ cup white chocolate chips

confectioners' sugar, to dust

1 Grease a 13 x 9 x 2 inch cake pan with a little butter or margarine.

2 Place all the ingredients in the order listed, except the chocolate chips and confectioners' sugar, in a large mixing bowl and beat together until smooth.

3 Beat in the milk, dark, and white chocolate chips.

4 Spoon the mixture into the prepared cake pan and level the surface. Bake in a preheated oven at 350°F for 30–40 minutes, until risen and springy to the touch. Cool in the pan.

5 Once cool, dust with confectioners' sugar. Cut into squares to serve.

COOK'S TIP

The cake can be frozen, wrapped in the pan, for 2 months. Thaw at room temperature.

COOK'S TIP

If desired, serve warm with cream for a delicious dessert.

VARIATION

For an attractive finish, cut thin strips of paper and lay in a criss-cross pattern on top of the cake. Dust with confectioners' sugar, then remove the paper strips.

Low-Fat Chocolate & Pineapple Cake

Serves 9

INGREDIENTS

²/₃ cup low-fat spread
4¹/₂ ounces superfine sugar
³/₄ cup self-rising flour, sifted
3 tbsp unsweetened cocoa, sifted

1¹/₂ tsp baking powder
2 eggs
8 ounce can pineapple pieces in natural juice

¹/₂ cup low-fat thick unsweetened yogurt
about 1 tbsp confectioners' sugar
grated chocolate, to decorate

1 Lightly grease an 8-inch square cake pan.

2 Place the low-fat spread, superfine sugar, flour, unsweetened cocoa, baking powder, and eggs in a large mixing bowl. Beat with a wooden spoon or electric beater until smooth.

3 Pour the cake mixture into the prepared pan and level the surface. Bake in a preheated oven at 325°F for 20–25 minutes, or until springy to the touch. Cool slightly in the pan before transferring to a wire rack to cool completely.

4 Drain the pineapple, chop the pineapple pieces, and drain again. Reserve a little of the pineapple for decoration, then stir the rest into the yogurt and sweeten to taste with confectioners' sugar.

5 Spread the pineapple and yogurt mixture over the cake and decorate with the reserved pineapple pieces. Sprinkle with the grated chocolate.

COOK'S TIP

Store the cake, undecorated, in an airtight container for up to 3 days. Once decorated, refrigerate and use within 2 days.

Chocolate & Orange Cake

Serves 8–10

INGREDIENTS

³⁄₄ cup superfine sugar	2 tbsp unsweetened cocoa, sifted	FROSTING:
³⁄₄ cup butter or margarine	2 tbsp milk	1 cup confectioners' sugar
3 eggs, beaten	3 tbsp orange juice	2 tbsp orange juice
1¹⁄₂ cups self-rising flour, sifted	grated rind of ¹⁄₂ orange	

1 Lightly grease a deep 8-inch round cake pan.

2 Beat together the sugar and butter or margarine in a bowl until light and fluffy. Gradually add the eggs, beating well after each addition. Carefully fold in the flour.

3 Divide the mixture in half. Add the unsweetened cocoa and milk to one half, stirring until combined. Flavor the other half with the orange juice and rind.

4 Spoon each mixture into the prepared pan and swirl together with a toothpick, to create a marbled effect. Bake in a preheated oven at 375°F for 25 minutes, or until springy to the touch.

5 Allow the cake to cool in the pan for a few minutes before transferring to a wire rack to cool completely.

6 To make the frosting, sift the confectioners' sugar into a mixing bowl and mix in enough of the orange juice to form a smooth frosting. Spread the frosting over the top of the cake and allow to set before serving.

VARIATION

Add 2 tablespoons of rum or brandy to the chocolate mixture instead of the milk. The cake also works well when flavored with grated lemon rind and juice.

Family Chocolate Cake

Serves 8–10

INGREDIENTS

¹/₂ cup soft margarine
²/₃ cup superfine sugar
2 eggs
1 tbsp light corn syrup
1 cup self-rising flour, sifted
2 tbsp unsweetened cocoa, sifted

FILLING AND TOPPING:
¹/₄ cup confectioners' sugar, sifted
2 tbsp butter
3¹/₂ ounces white or milk chocolate
a little milk or white chocolate,
    melted (optional)

1 Lightly grease two shallow 7-inch cake pans.

2 Place all the ingredients for the cake in a large mixing bowl and beat with a wooden spoon or electric mixer to form a smooth mixture.

3 Divide the mixture between the prepared pans and level the tops. Bake in a preheated oven at 325°F for 20 minutes, or until springy to the touch. Cool for a few minutes in the pans before transferring to a wire rack to cool completely.

4 To make the filling, beat the confectioners' sugar and butter together in a bowl until light and fluffy. Melt the chocolate and beat half into the frosting mixture. Use the filling to sandwich the cakes together.

5 Spread the remaining melted cooking chocolate over the top of the cake. Pipe circles of contrasting melted milk or white chocolate and feather into the chocolate with a toothpick, if preferred. Allow to set before serving.

COOK'S TIP

Eat this cake on the day of baking, as it does not keep well.

Chocolate & Vanilla Loaf Cake

Serves 10

INGREDIENTS

³/₄ cup superfine sugar
³/₄ cup soft margarine
¹/₂ tsp vanilla extract
3 eggs

2 cups self-rising flour, sifted
1³/₄ ounces dark chocolate
confectioners' sugar, to dust

1 Lightly grease a 1-pound loaf pan.

2 Beat together the sugar and soft margarine in a bowl until light and fluffy.

3 Beat in the vanilla extract. Gradually add the eggs, beating thoroughly after each addition. Carefully fold in the sifted flour.

4 Divide the mixture in half. Melt the dark chocolate and stir into one half of the mixture until well combined.

5 Place the vanilla mixture in the pan and level the top. Spread the chocolate layer over the vanilla layer.

6 Bake in a preheated oven at 375°F for 30 minutes, or until springy to the touch.

7 Cool the cake in the pan for a few minutes before transferring to a wire rack to cool completely.

8 Serve the cake lightly dusted with a little confectioners' sugar, if you wish.

COOK'S TIP

Freeze the cake undecorated for up to 2 months. Thaw at room temperature.

VARIATION

If desired, the mixtures can be marbled together with a toothpick.

Chocolate Tea Bread

Serves 10

INGREDIENTS

³/₄ cup butter, softened
½ cup light brown sugar
4 eggs, lightly beaten
8 ounces dark chocolate chips

½ cup raisins
½ cup chopped walnuts

finely grated rind of 1 orange
2 cups self-rising flour

---

1 Lightly grease a 2-pound loaf pan and line the base with baking parchment.

2 Cream together the butter and sugar in a bowl until light and fluffy.

3 Gradually add the eggs, beating well after each addition. If the mixture begins to curdle, beat in 1-2 tablespoons of the flour.

4 Stir in the chocolate chips, raisins, walnuts, and orange rind. Sift the flour and carefully fold it into the mixture.

5 Spoon the mixture into the prepared loaf pan and make a slight dip in the center of the top with the back of a spoon.

6 Bake in a preheated oven at 325°F for about 1 hour, or until a toothpick inserted into the center of the loaf comes out clean.

7 Cool in the pan for 5 minutes before carefully turning out and leaving on a wire rack to cool completely.

8 Serve the sweet bread cut into thin slices.

VARIATION

Use white or milk chocolate chips instead of dark chocolate chips, or a mixture of all three, if desired. Dried cranberries instead of the raisins also work well in this recipe.

COOK'S TIP

This sweet bread can be frozen, well wrapped, for up to 3 months. Thaw at room temperature.

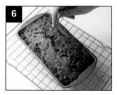

Apricot & Chocolate Ring

Serves 12

INGREDIENTS

⅓ cup butter, diced
4 cups self-rising flour, sifted
4 tbsp superfine sugar
2 eggs, beaten
⅔ cup milk

FILLING AND DECORATION:
2 tbsp butter, melted
⅔ cup no-need-to-soak dried
    apricots, chopped
3½ ounces dark chocolate chips
1–2 tbsp milk, to glaze

1 ounce dark chocolate, melted

1 Grease a 10-inch round cake pan and line the base with baking parchment.

2 Rub the butter into the flour until the mixture resembles fine breadcrumbs. Stir in the superfine sugar, eggs, and milk to form a soft dough.

3 Roll out the dough on a lightly floured surface to form a 14-inch square.

4 Brush the melted butter over the surface of the dough. Mix together the apricots and chocolate chips and spread them over the dough to within 1 inch of the top and bottom.

5 Roll up the dough tightly, like a jelly roll, and cut it into 1-inch slices. Stand the slices in a ring around the edge of the prepared pan at a slight tilt. Brush with a little milk.

6 Bake in a preheated oven at 350°F for 30 minutes, or until cooked and golden. Cool the cake in the pan for about 15 minutes, then carefully transfer to a wire rack to cool.

7 Drizzle the melted chocolate over the ring, to decorate.

COOK'S TIP

This cake is best served very fresh, ideally on the day it is made. It is fabulous served slightly warm.

Chocolate Fruit Loaf

Serves 10

INGREDIENTS

---

3 cups strong white flour

1/4 cup unsweetened cocoa

5 tsp superfine sugar

1 envelope active dry yeast

1/4 tsp salt

1 cup tepid water

2 tbsp butter, melted

5 tbsp candied cherries,
    roughly chopped

1/2 cup dark chocolate chips

1/3 cup golden raisins

3/4 cup no-need-to soak dried
    apricots, roughly chopped

GLAZE:

1 tbsp superfine sugar

1 tbsp water

---

1 Lightly grease a
2-pound loaf pan.
Sift the flour and cocoa into
a large mixing bowl. Stir in
the sugar, yeast, and salt.

2 Mix together the tepid
water and butter.
Make a well in the center
of the dry ingredients
and add the liquid. Mix
well with a wooden
spoon, then use your hands
to bring the dough together.
Turn out onto a lightly
floured surface and knead
for 5 minutes, until

a smooth elastic dough
forms. Return to a clean
bowl, cover with a damp
dish cloth, and set aside
to rise in a warm place
for about 1 hour, or until
doubled in size.

3 Turn the dough out
onto a floured surface
and knead for 5 minutes.
Roll out to a rectangle about
1/2 inch thick and the same
width as the length of
the pan. Scatter the cherries,
chocolate chips, golden
raisins, and chopped apricots

over the dough. Carefully
roll up the dough, like
a jelly roll, enclosing the
filling. Transfer to the loaf
pan, cover with a damp dish
cloth, and set aside to rise
for 20 minutes, or until the
top of the dough is level
with the top of the pan.

4 To make the glaze,
mix together the sugar
and water, then brush it
over the top of the loaf.
Bake in a preheated oven
at 400°F for 30 minutes, or
until well risen. Serve warm.

Mocha Layer Cake

Serves 8–10

INGREDIENTS

2 cups self-rising flour
1/4 tsp baking powder
4 tbsp unsweetened cocoa
7 tbsp superfine sugar
2 eggs
2 tbsp light corn syrup
2/3 cup sunflower oil
2/3 cup milk

FILLING:
1 tsp instant coffee
1 tbsp boiling water
1 1/4 cups heavy cream
2 tbsp confectioners' sugar

TO DECORATE:
1 3/4 ounces dark chocolate to make curls
chocolate caraque
confectioners' sugar, to dust

1 Lightly grease three 7-inch cake pans.

2 Sift the flour, baking powder, and unsweetened cocoa into a large mixing bowl. Stir in the sugar. Make a well in the center and stir in the eggs, syrup, oil, and milk. Beat with a wooden spoon, gradually mixing in the dry ingredients to make a smooth batter. Divide the mixture between the prepared pans.

3 Bake in a preheated oven at 350°F for 35–45 minutes, or until springy to the touch. Leave the cakes in the pans for 5 minutes, then turn out onto a wire rack to cool completely.

4 Dissolve the instant coffee in the boiling water and place in a bowl with the cream and confectioners' sugar. Whip until the cream is just holding its shape. Use half the cream to sandwich the 3 cakes together. Spread the remaining cream over the top and sides of the cake. Lightly press the chocolate curls into the cream around the edge of the cake.

5 Transfer to a serving plate. Lay the caraque over the top of the cake. Cut a few thin strips of baking parchment and place on top of the caraque. Dust lightly with confectioners' sugar, then carefully remove the paper. Serve.

Chocolate Lamington Pound Cake

Serves 8–10

INGREDIENTS

³⁄₄ cup butter or margarine
³⁄₄ cup superfine sugar
3 eggs, lightly beaten
1¹⁄₄ cups self-rising flour

2 tbsp unsweetened cocoa
1³⁄₄ ounces dark chocolate, broken
    into pieces
5 tbsp milk

1 tsp butter
³⁄₄ cup confectioners' sugar
about 8 tbsp shredded coconut
²⁄₃ cup heavy cream, whipped

1 Lightly grease a 1-pound loaf pan—preferably a long, thin pan about 3 x 10 inches.

2 Cream together the butter and sugar in a bowl until light and fluffy. Gradually add the eggs, beating well after each addition. Sift together the flour and cocoa. Fold into the mixture.

3 Pour the mixture into the prepared pan and level the top. Bake in a preheated oven at 350°F for 40 minutes, or until springy to the touch. Cool the cake for 5 minutes in the pan, then turn out onto a wire rack to cool completely.

4 Place the chocolate, milk, and butter in a double boiler. Stir until the chocolate has melted. Add the confectioners' sugar and beat until smooth. Cool until the frosting is thick enough to spread, then spread it all over the cake. Sprinkle with the shredded coconut and allow the frosting to set.

5 Cut a V-shape wedge from the top of the cake and set aside. Put the cream in a pastry bag fitted with a plain or star tip. Pipe the cream down the center of the V-shaped gap and replace the wedge of cake on top of the cream. Pipe another line of cream along either side of the wedge of cake. Serve.

Rich Chocolate Layer Cake

Serves 10–12

INGREDIENTS

7 eggs
1³/₄ cups superfine sugar
1¹/₄ cups all-purpose flour
¹/₂ cup unsweetened cocoa
4 tbsp butter, melted

FILLING:
7 ounces dark chocolate
¹/₂ cup butter
4 tbsp confectioners' sugar

TO DECORATE:
²/₃ cup toasted slivered almonds,
  lightly crushed
small chocolate curls or grated
  chocolate

1 Grease a deep 9-inch square cake pan and line the base with baking parchment.

2 Beat the eggs and superfine sugar in a mixing bowl with an electric beater for about 10 minutes, or until the mixture is very light and foamy and the beater leaves a trail that lasts a few seconds when lifted.

3 Sift the flour and cocoa together and fold half into the mixture.

Drizzle the melted butter over it and fold in the rest of the flour and cocoa. Pour into the prepared pan and bake in a preheated oven at 350°F for 30–35 minutes, or until springy to the touch. Cool slightly, then remove from the pan and cool completely on a wire rack.

4 To make the filling, melt the chocolate and butter together, then remove from the heat. Stir in the confectioners' sugar,

let cool, then beat until thick enough to spread.

5 Halve the cake length-wise and cut each half into 3 layers. Sandwich the layers together with three-quarters of the chocolate filling. Spread the remainder over the cake and mark a wavy pattern on the top. Press the almonds onto the sides. Decorate with chocolate curls or grated chocolate.

Chocolate & Mango Layer Cake

Serves 12

INGREDIENTS

1/2 cup unsweetened cocoa	2 1/2 cups self-rising flour	2 3/4 ounces dark chocolate, curled,
2/3 cup boiling water	2 x 14 ounce cans mango	or grated chocolate
6 large eggs	1 tsp cornstarch	
1 1/2 cups superfine sugar	1 3/4 cups heavy cream	

1 Grease a deep 9-inch round cake pan and line the base with baking parchment.

2 Place the unsweetened cocoa in a small bowl and gradually add the boiling water; blend to form a smooth paste.

3 Place the eggs and superfine sugar in a mixing bowl and beat until the mixture is very light and foamy and the beater leaves a trail that lasts a few seconds when lifted. Fold in the cocoa mixture. Sift the flour and carefully fold it into the mixture.

4 Pour the mixture into the pan and level the top. Bake in a preheated oven at 325°F for about 1 hour or until springy to the touch.

5 Cool in the pan for a few minutes, then turn out and cool completely on a wire rack. Peel off the lining paper and cut the cake into 3 layers.

6 Drain the mangoes and place a quarter them in a food processor and process until smooth. Mix the cornstarch with about 3 tbsp of the mango juice to form a smooth paste.

Add to the mango purée. Transfer to a small pan and heat gently, stirring until the purée thickens. Let cool.

7 Chop the remaining mango. Whip the cream and reserve about one quarter. Fold the mango into the remaining cream and use to sandwich the layers of cake together. Place on a serving plate. Spread some of the remaining cream around the side of the cake. Press the curled or grated chocolate lightly into the cream. Pipe cream rosettes around the top. Spread the mango purée over the center.

Devil's Food Cake

Serves 8

INGREDIENTS

3¹/₂ ounces dark chocolate	1 tsp vanilla extract	FROSTING:
2¹/₄ cups self-rising flour	3 eggs	1¹/₃ cups superfine sugar
1 tsp baking soda	¹/₂ cup buttermilk	2 egg whites
1 cup butter	2 cups boiling water	1 tbsp lemon juice
2²/₃ cups dark brown sugar		3 tbsp orange juice
		candied orange peel, to decorate

1 Lightly grease and flour two shallow 8-inch round cake pans. Melt the chocolate in a pan. Sift the flour and baking soda together.

2 Beat the butter and dark brown sugar in a bowl until pale and fluffy. Beat in the vanilla extract and the eggs, one at a time and beating well after each addition. Add a little extra flour if the mixture is beginning to curdle.

3 Fold the melted chocolate into the mixture until well blended. Gradually fold in the remaining flour, then stir in the buttermilk and boiling water.

4 Divide the mixture between the pans and level the tops. Bake in a preheated oven at 375°F for 30 minutes, until springy to the touch. Cool the cakes in the pans for 5 minutes, then transfer to a wire rack to cool completely.

5 Place the frosting ingredients in a double boiler over gently simmering water. Beat, preferably with an electric beater, until thickened and forming soft peaks. Remove from the heat and beat until the mixture is cool.

6 Sandwich the 2 cakes together with a little of the frosting, then spread the remainder over the sides and top of the cake, swirling it as you do so. Decorate with the candied orange peel.

Chocolate Carrot Cake

Serves 10–12

INGREDIENTS

5 eggs
²/₃ cup superfine sugar
1¼ cups all-purpose flour
⅓ cup unsweetened cocoa

6 ounces carrots, peeled and finely grated
½ cup chopped walnuts
2 tbsp sunflower oil

12 ounces cream cheese
1 cup confectioners' sugar
6 ounces milk or dark chocolate, melted

1 Lightly grease and flour the base of a deep 8-inch round cake pan.

2 Place the eggs and sugar in a double boiler over gently simmering water and beat until very thick. Lift the whisk up and let the mixture drizzle back – it will leave a trail for a few seconds when thick enough.

3 Remove from the heat. Sift the flour and unsweetened cocoa into the mixture and carefully fold in. Gently fold in the carrots, walnuts, and oil until just combined.

4 Pour into the prepared pan and bake in a preheated oven at 375°F for 45 minutes, or until well risen and springy to the touch. Cool the cake slightly, then turn out onto a wire rack to cool completely.

5 Beat together the cheese and confectioners' sugar until combined. Beat in the melted chocolate. Split the cake in half and sandwich together again with half the chocolate mixture. Cover the top of the cake with the remainder of the chocolate mixture, swirling it with a knife. Chill or serve at once.

COOK'S TIP

The undecorated cake can be frozen for up to 2 months. Thaw at room temperature for 3 hours or overnight in the refrigerator.

Chocolate Yogurt Cake

Serves 8–10

INGREDIENTS

²/₃ cup vegetable oil
²/₃ cup whole milk
    unsweetened yogurt
1¼ cups light brown sugar
3 eggs, beaten
³/₄ cup whole-wheat self-rising
    flour1 cup self-rising flour,
    sifted

2 tbsp unsweetened cocoa
1 tsp baking soda
1³/₄ ounces dark chocolate, melted

FILLING:
²/₃ cup whole milk
    unsweetened yogurt
²/₃ cup heavy cream
8 ounces fresh soft fruit, such as
    strawberries or raspberries

1 Grease a deep 9-inch round cake pan and line the base with baking parchment.

2 Place the oil, yogurt, sugar, and beaten eggs in a large mixing bowl and beat together until well combined. Sift the flours, unsweetened cocoa, and baking soda together and beat into the bowl until thoroughly combined. Beat in the melted dark chocolate.

3 Pour the mixture into the prepared pan and bake in a preheated oven at 350°F for 45–50 minutes, or until a toothpick inserted into the center comes out clean. Cool in the pan for 5 minutes, then turn out onto a wire rack to cool completely. When cold, divide the cake into 3 layers.

4 Place the yogurt and cream in a large mixing bowl and beat well until the mixture stands in soft peaks.

5 Place one layer of cake onto a serving plate and spread with some of the cream. Top with a little of the fruit (slicing larger fruit such as strawberries). Repeat with the next layer. Top with the final layer of cake and spread with the rest of the cream. Arrange more fruit on top and cut the cake into wedges to serve.

Chocolate Layer Log

Serves 8–10

INGREDIENTS

¹/₂ cup soft margarine
¹/₂ cup superfine sugar
2 eggs
³/₄ cup self-rising flour
¹/₄ cup unsweetened cocoa
2 tbsp milk

WHITE CHOCOLATE BUTTER CREAM:
2³/₄ ounces white chocolate
2 tbsp milk
²/₃ cup butter ³/₄ cup confectioners'
    sugar
2 tbsp orange-flavored liqueur

large dark chocolate curls
to decorate

1 Grease and flour the sides of two clean, dry 14-ounce food cans.

2 Beat together the margarine and sugar in a bowl until light and fluffy. Gradually add the eggs, beating well after each addition. Sift together the flour and unsweetened cocoa and fold into the cake mixture. Fold in the milk.

3 Divide the mixture between the two prepared cans. Stand the cans on a cookie sheet and bake in a preheated oven at 350°F for 40 minutes, or until springy to the touch. Cool the cakes for about 5 minutes in the cans, then turn out and cool completely on a wire rack.

4 To make the butter cream, put the chocolate and milk in a pan and heat gently until the chocolate has melted, stirring until well combined. Let cool slightly. Beat together the butter and confectioners' sugar until light and fluffy. Beat in the orange liqueur.

Gradually beat in the chocolate mixture.

5 To assemble, cut both cakes into ¹/₂-inch-thick slices, then reassemble them by sandwiching the slices together with some of the butter cream.

6 Place the cake on a serving plate and spread the remaining butter cream over the top and sides. Decorate with the chocolate curls, then serve the cake cut diagonally into slices.

Chocolate & Orange Mousse Cake

Serves 12

INGREDIENTS

³/₄ cup butter
³/₄ cup superfine sugar
4 eggs, lightly beaten
1³/₄ cups self-raising flour
1 tbsp cocoa powder
1³/₄ oz dark orange-flavoured
chocolate, melted

ORANGE MOUSSE:
2 eggs, separated
4 tbsp superfine sugar
³/₄ cup freshly squeezed orange
juice
2 tsp gelatine
3 tbsp water

¹/₄ cups heavy cream
peeled orange slices, to decorate

1 Grease a 20 cm/8 inch springform cake pan and and line the base. Beat the butter and sugar in a bowl until light and fluffy. Gradually add the eggs, beating well after each addition. strain together the cocoa and flour and fold into the cake mixture. Fold in the chocolate.

2 Pour into the prepared pan and level the top. Bake in a preheated oven, 180°C/350°F/Gas Mark 4, for 40 minutes or until springy to the touch.

Leave to cool for 5 minutes in the pan, then turn out and leave to cool completely on a wire rack. Cut the cold cake into 2 layers.

3 To make the orange mousse, beat the egg yolks and sugar until light, then whisk in the orange juice. Sprinkle the gelatine over the water in a small bowl and allow to go spongy, then place over a pan of hot water and stir until dissolved. Stir into the mousse.

4 Whip the cream until holding its shape, reserve a little for decoration and fold the rest into the mousse. Whisk the egg whites until standing in soft peaks, then fold in. Leave in a cool place until starting to set, stirring occasionally.

5 Place half of the cake in the pan. Pour in the mousse and press the second cake layer on top. Chill until set. Transfer to a dish, pipe cream rosettes on the top and arrange orange slices in the center.

Chocolate Roulade

Serves 6–8

INGREDIENTS

5¹/₂ ounces dark chocolate
2 tbsp water
6 eggs
³/₄ cup superfine sugar
¹/₄ cup all-purpose flour
1 tbsp unsweetened cocoa

FILLING:
1¹/₄ cups heavy cream
2³/₄ ounces sliced strawberries

TO DECORATE:
confectioners' sugar
chocolate leaves (see below)

1 Line a 15 x 10 inch jelly roll pan with baking parchment. Melt the chocolate in the water, stirring. Let cool slightly.

2 Place the eggs and sugar in a bowl and beat for 10 minutes, or until the mixture is pale and foamy and the beater leaves a trail when lifted. Beat in the melted chocolate in a thin stream. Sift the flour and cocoa together and fold into the mixture. Pour into the pan and level the top.

3 Bake in a preheated oven at 400°F for 12 minutes. Dust a sheet of baking parchment with a little confectioners' sugar. Turn out the roulade and remove the lining paper. Roll up the roulade with the fresh parchment inside. Place on a wire rack, cover with a damp dish cloth, and let cool.

4 Beat the cream until just holding its shape. Unroll the roulade, remove the paper, and scatter the fruit over it. Spread three quarters of the cream over

the roulade and re-roll. Dust with confectioners' sugar. Place the roulade on a plate. Pipe the rest of the cream down the center and decorate with chocolate leaves.

5 To make chocolate leaves, wash some rose or holly leaves and pat dry with paper towels. Melt some chocolate and brush it over the leaves. Set aside to harden. Repeat with 2–3 layers of chocolate. Peel the leaves away from the chocolate.

Chocolate & Coconut Roulade

Serves 8–10

INGREDIENTS

3 eggs
1/3 cup superfine sugar
1/3 cup self-rising flour
1 tbsp block creamed coconut,
    softened with 1 tbsp boiling water
1 cup shredded coconut
6 tbsp good raspberry conserve

CHOCOLATE COATING:
7 ounces dark chocolate
1/4 cup butter
2 tbsp light corn syrup

RASPBERRY COULIS:
1 1/3 cups fresh or frozen raspberries,
    thawed if frozen
2 tbsp water
4 tbsp confectioners' sugar

1 Grease and line a 9 x 12 inch jelly roll pan. Beat together the eggs and superfine sugar in a large mixing bowl with an electric mixer for about 10 minutes, or until the mixture is very light and foamy and the beater leaves a trail that will last a few seconds when lifted.

2 Sift the flour and fold in with a metal spoon or a spatula. Fold in the creamed coconut and shredded coconut.

Pour into the prepared pan and bake in a preheated oven at 400°F for about 10–12 minutes, or until springy to the touch.

3 Sprinkle a sheet of baking parchment with a little superfine sugar and place on top of a damp dish cloth. Turn the cake out onto the paper and carefully peel away the lining paper. Spread the conserve over the sponge cake and roll up from the short end, using the dish cloth to help you. Place seam

side down on a wire rack and cool completely.

4 To make the coating, melt the chocolate and butter, stirring constantly. Stir in the light corn syrup and set aside to cool for 5 minutes. Spread it over the roulade and allow to set. To make the coulis, purée the fruit in a food processor with the water and sugar; run through a strainer to remove the seeds. Cut the roulade into slices and serve with the coulis.

Almond & Hazelnut Cake

Serves 8–10

INGREDIENTS

4 eggs
7 tbsp superfine sugar
$1/2$ cup ground almonds
$1/2$ cup ground hazelnuts
$1/3$ cup all-purpose flour
$1/2$ cup slivered almonds

FILLING:
$3^1/2$ ounces dark chocolate
1 tbsp butter
$1^1/4$ cups heavy cream
confectioners' sugar, to dust

1 Grease two 7-inch round sponge cake layer pans and line the bases with sheets of baking parchment.

2 Beat the eggs and superfine sugar together in a large mixing bowl with an electric mixer for about 10 minutes, or until the mixture is very light and foamy and the beater leaves a trail that lasts a few seconds when lifted.

3 Fold in the ground nuts, sift the flour and fold in with a metal spoon or spatula. Pour into the prepared pans.

4 Scatter the slivered almonds over the top of one of the cakes. Bake both cakes in a preheated oven at 375°F for 15–20 minutes, or until springy to the touch.

5 Cool the cakes slightly in the pans. Carefully remove the cakes from the pans and transfer them to a wire rack to cool completely.

6 To make the filling, melt the chocolate, remove from the heat, and stir in the butter. Let cool slightly. Whip the cream until just holding its shape, then fold in the melted chocolate until mixed.

7 Place the cake without the extra almonds on a serving plate and spread the filling over it. Allow to set slightly, then place the almond-topped cake on top of the filling and chill for about 1 hour. Dust with confectioners' sugar and serve.

Chocolate & Walnut Cake

Serves 8–12

INGREDIENTS

4 eggs	2 tbsp butter, melted	FROSTING:
$^1/_2$ cup superfine sugar	$2^3/_4$ ounces dark chocolate, melted	$2^3/_4$ ounces dark chocolate
1 cup all-purpose flour	$1^1/_4$ cups finely chopped walnuts	$^1/_2$ cup butter
1 tbsp unsweetened cocoa		$1^1/_4$ cups confectioners' sugar
		2 tbsp milk
		walnut halves, to decorate

1 Grease a deep 7-inch round cake pan and line the base. Place the eggs and superfine sugar in a mixing bowl and beat with an electric mixer for 10 minutes, or until the mixture is light and foamy and the beater leaves a trail that lasts a few seconds when lifted.

2 Sift together the flour and unsweetened cocoa and fold in with a metal spoon or spatula. Fold in the melted butter and chocolate,

and the chopped walnuts. Pour into the prepared pan and bake in a preheated oven at 325°F for 30–35 minutes, or until springy to the touch.

3 Cool the cake in the pan for 5 minutes, then transfer to a wire rack to cool completely. Cut the cold cake into 2 layers.

4 To make the frosting, melt the dark chocolate and let cool slightly. Beat together the butter, confectioners' sugar,

and milk in a bowl until the mixture is pale and fluffy. Beat in the melted chocolate.

5 Sandwich the 2 cake layers with some of the frosting and then transfer to a serving plate. Spread the remaining frosting over the top of the cake with a spatula, swirling it slightly as you do so to make a pattern. Decorate the cake with the walnut halves and serve.

Dobos Torte

Serves 8

INGREDIENTS

3 eggs
7 tbsp superfine sugar
1 tsp vanilla extract
1/2 cup all-purpose flour

FILLING:
6 ounces dark chocolate
3/4 cup butter
2 tbsp milk
2 cups confectioners' sugar

CARAMEL:
7 tbsp sugar
4 tbsp water

1 Draw four 7-inch circles on sheets of baking parchment. Place 2 of them upside down on 2 cookie sheets. Beat the eggs and superfine sugar in a large mixing bowl with an electric mixer for 10 minutes, or until the mixture is light and foamy and the beater leaves a trail that lasts for a few seconds when lifted. Fold in the vanilla extract. Sift the flour and fold in with a metal spoon or a spatula. Spoon a quarter of the mixture onto one of the sheets and spread out to the size of the circle. Repeat with the other circle. Bake in a preheated oven at 400°F for 5–8 minutes, or until golden brown. Cool on wire racks. Repeat with the remaining mixture.

2 To make the filling, melt the chocolate and cool slightly. Beat the butter, milk, and confectioners' sugar until pale and fluffy. Beat in the chocolate. Place the sugar and water for the caramel in a heavy-based pan and heat gently, stirring until the sugar dissolves. Boil gently until the syrup is pale golden. Remove the pan from the heat. Pour the caramel over one layer of the cake to cover the top. Allow to harden slightly, then mark into 8 portions with an oiled knife. Remove the cakes from the paper and trim the edges. Sandwich the layers together with some of the filling, finishing with the caramel-topped cake. Place on a serving plate and spread the sides with the filling mixture. Pipe rosettes around the top of the cake. Cut into slices to serve.

Bistvitny Torte

Serves 10

INGREDIENTS

CHOCOLATE TRIANGLES:
1 ounce dark chocolate, melted
1 ounce white chocolate, melted

CAKE:
$^3/_4$ cup soft margarine

$^3/_4$ cup superfine sugar
$^1/_2$ tsp vanilla extract
3 eggs, lightly beaten
2 cups self-rising flour
$1^3/_4$ ounces dark chocolate

SYRUP:
$^1/_2$ cup sugar
6 tbsp water
3 tbsp brandy or sherry
$^2/_3$ cup heavy cream

1 Grease a 9-inch ring pan. To make the triangles, place a sheet of baking parchment onto a cookie sheet and place alternate spoonfuls of the dark and white chocolate onto the paper. Spread together to form a thick marbled layer. Allow to set. Cut into squares, then into triangles.

2 To make the cake, beat the margarine and sugar until light and fluffy. Beat in the vanilla extract. Gradually add the eggs, beating well after each addition.

Carefully fold in the flour. Divide the mixture in half. Melt the dark chocolate and stir into one half.

3 Spoon each mixture into the prepared pan and swirl together with a toothpick to create a marbled effect.

4 Bake in a preheated oven at 375°F for 30 minutes, or until the cake is springy to the touch. Cool in the pan for a few minutes, then transfer to a wire rack to cool completely.

5 To make the syrup, place the sugar in a small pan with the water and heat, stirring until the sugar has dissolved. Boil for 1–2 minutes. Remove the pan from the heat and stir in the brandy or sherry. Let the syrup cool slightly then gradually spoon it over the cake, allowing it to soak into the sponge cake. Whip the cream and pipe swirls of it on top of the cake. Finally, decorate with the chocolate triangles.

Sachertorte

Serves 10–12

INGREDIENTS

6 ounces dark chocolate
²/₃ cup sweet butter
²/₃ cup superfine sugar
6 eggs, separated
1¼ cups all-purpose flour

FROSTING AND FILLING:
6 ounces dark chocolate
5 tbsp strong black coffee1 cup
   confectioners' sugar

6 tbsp apricot preserve
1³/₄ ounces dark chocolate, melted

1 Grease a 9-inch springform cake pan and flour the base. Melt the chocolate. Beat the butter and ²/₃ cup of the sugar until pale and fluffy. Add the egg yolks and beat. Add the chocolate in a thin continuous stream, beating well. Sift the flour and fold it into the mixture. Beat the egg whites until they stand in soft peaks. Add the remaining sugar and whisk for 2 minutes by hand, or 45-60 seconds with an electric mixer, until glossy. Fold half into the chocolate mixture, then fold in the remainder.

2 Spoon into the prepared pan and level the top. Bake in a preheated oven at 300°F for 1–1¼ hours, until a toothpick inserted into the center comes out clean. Cool the cake in the pan for 5 minutes, then transfer to a wire rack to cool completely.

3 To make the frosting, melt the chocolate and beat in the coffee until smooth. Sift the confectioners' sugar into a bowl. Beat in the chocolate mixture to make a thick frosting. Halve the cake. Warm the preserve, spread over one half of the cake, and

sandwich together. Invert the cake on a wire rack. Spoon the frosting over the cake and spread to coat the top and sides. Allow to set for 5 minutes, allowing any excess frosting to drop through the rack. Transfer to a serving plate and allow to set for at least 2 hours.

4 To decorate, spoon the melted chocolate into a small pastry bag and pipe the word "Sacher" or "Sachertorte" on the top of the cake. Allow it to harden before serving.

Dark & White Chocolate Torte

Serves 10

INGREDIENTS

4 eggs
1/2 cup superfine sugar
3/4 cup all-purpose flour

DARK CHOCOLATE CREAM:
2/3 cup heavy cream
5 1/2 ounces dark chocolate, broken
　　into small pieces

WHITE CHOCOLATE FROSTING:
2 3/4 ounces white chocolate
1 tbsp butter
1 tbsp milk
4 tbsp confectioners' sugar
chocolate caraque

1 Grease an 8-inch round springform pan and line the base. Beat the eggs and superfine sugar in a large mixing bowl with an electric mixer for about 10 minutes, or until the mixture is very light and foamy and the beater leaves a trail that lasts a few seconds when lifted.

2 Sift the flour and fold in with a metal spoon or spatula. Pour into the prepared pan and bake in a preheated oven at 350°F for 35–40 minutes, or until springy to the touch. Cool the cake slightly in the pan, then transfer to a wire rack to cool completely. Cut the cold cake into 2 layers.

3 To make the chocolate cream, place the cream in a saucepan and bring to a boil, stirring. Add the chocolate and stir until melted and well combined. Remove from the heat and let cool. Beat with a wooden spoon until the mixture starts to thicken.

4 Sandwich the 2 cake layers together with the chocolate cream and place on a wire rack.

5 To make the frosting, melt the chocolate and butter together and stir until thoroughly blended. Beat in the milk and confectioners' sugar. Beat for a few minutes, until the frosting is cool. Pour it over the cake and spread with a spatula to coat the top and sides. Decorate with chocolate caraque and allow to set.

Chocolate Ganache Cake

Serves 10–12

INGREDIENTS

³/₄ cup butter
³/₄ cup superfine sugar
4 eggs, lightly beaten
1³/₄ cups self-rising flour
1 tbsp unsweetened cocoa
1³/₄ ounces dark chocolate, melted

GANACHE:
2 cups heavy cream
13 ounces dark chocolate, broken
    into pieces

TO FINISH:
7 ounces chocolate-flavored cake
    covering or dark chocolate

1 Lightly grease an 8-inch springform cake pan and flour the base. Beat the butter and sugar until light and fluffy. Gradually add the eggs, beating well after each addition. Sift together the flour and cocoa. Carefully fold into the cake mixture. Fold in the melted chocolate.

2 Pour into the prepared pan and level the top. Bake in a preheated oven at 350°F for 40 minutes, or until just springy to the touch. Allow the cake to cool for 5 minutes in the pan,

then turn out onto a wire rack to cool completely. Cut the cold cake into 2 layers.

3 To make the ganache, place the cream in a pan and bring to a boil, stirring. Add the chocolate and stir until melted and combined. Pour into a bowl and beat for about 5 minutes, or until the ganache is fluffy and cool.

4 Reserve one-third of the ganache. Use the remaining ganache to sandwich the cake layers together and to

spread over the top and sides of the cake.

5 Melt the cake covering or chocolate and spread it over a large sheet of baking parchment. Cool until just set. Cut into strips a little wider than the height of the cake and place around the edge of the cake, overlapping them slightly.

6 Pipe the reserved ganache in tear drops or shells over the top of the cake. Chill for 1 hour.

Yule Log

Serves 8–10

INGREDIENTS

CAKE:
4 eggs
$\frac{1}{2}$ cup superfine sugar
$\frac{2}{3}$ cup self-rising flour
2 tbsp unsweetened cocoa

FROSTING:
$5\frac{1}{2}$ ounces dark chocolate
2 egg yolks
$\frac{2}{3}$ cup milk
$\frac{1}{2}$ cup butter
4 tbsp confectioners' sugar
2 tbsp rum (optional)

TO DECORATE:
a little white glacé or royal frosting
confectioners' sugar, to dust
holly or Christmas cake decorations

1 Grease and line a 12 x 9 inch jelly roll pan. Beat the eggs and superfine sugar in a bowl with an electric mixer for 10 minutes, or until the mixture is very light and foamy and the beater leaves a trail. Sift the flour and unsweetened cocoa and fold in. Pour into the prepared pan and bake in a preheated oven at 400°F for 12 minutes, or until springy to the touch. Turn out onto a piece of baking parchment sprinkled with a little superfine sugar.

Peel off the lining paper and trim the edges. Cut a small slit halfway into the cake about $\frac{1}{2}$ inch from one short end. Starting at that end, roll up tightly, enclosing the paper. Place on a wire rack to cool.

2 To make the frosting, break the chocolate into pieces and melt in a double boiler. Beat in the egg yolks, then beat in the milk, and cook, stirring, until the mixture thickens enough to coat the back of a wooden spoon.

Cover with dampened wax paper and cool. Beat the butter and sugar until pale and fluffy. Beat in the cooled mixture and rum, if using. Unroll the sponge cake, remove the paper, spread with one third of the frosting, and roll up again. Place on a serving plate. Spread the remaining frosting over the cake and mark with a fork to give the effect of bark. Allow to set. Pipe white frosting to form the rings of the log. Sprinkle with sugar and decorate.

Chocolate Truffle Cake

Serves 12

INGREDIENTS
---

¹/₃ cup butter
¹/₃ cup superfine sugar
2 eggs, lightly beaten
²/₃ cup self-rising flour
¹/₂ tsp baking powder
¹/₄ cup unsweetened cocoa
¹/₂ cup ground almonds

TRUFFLE TOPPING:
12 ounces dark chocolate
¹/₂ cup butter
1¹/₄ cups heavy cream
1¹/₄ cups plain cake crumbs
3 tbsp dark rum

TO DECORATE:
ground cherries
1³/₄ ounces dark chocolate, melted

---

1 Lightly grease an 8-inch round springform pan and flour the base. Beat together the butter and sugar until light and fluffy. Gradually add the eggs, beating well after each addition.

2 Sift the flour, baking powder, and unsweetened cocoa together and fold into the mixture, along with the ground almonds. Pour into the prepared pan and bake in a preheated oven at 350°F for 20–25 minutes, or until springy to the touch. Cool the cake slightly in the pan, then transfer to a wire rack to cool completely. Wash and dry the pan and return the cooled cake to it.

3 To make the topping, heat the chocolate, butter, and heavy cream in a heavy-based pan over a low heat and stir until smooth. Cool, then chill for 30 minutes. Beat well with a wooden spoon and chill for a further 30 minutes. Beat the mixture again, then add the cake crumbs and rum, beating until well combined. Spoon the topping over the sponge cake base and chill for 3 hours.

4 Meanwhile, dip the ground cherries in the melted chocolate until partially covered. Set on baking parchment. Transfer the cake to a serving plate; decorate with ground cherries.

White Chocolate Truffle Cake

Serves 12

| INGREDIENTS |

2 eggs
4 tbsp superfine sugar
¹/₃ cup all-purpose flour
1³/₄ ounces white chocolate, melted

TRUFFLE TOPPING:
1¹/₄ cups heavy cream
12 ounces white chocolate, broken into pieces
1¹/₄ cups cream cheese

TO DECORATE:
dark, milk, or white chocolate, melted
unsweetened cocoa, to dust

1 Grease an 8-inch round springform pan and flour the base. Beat the eggs and superfine sugar in a mixing bowl for 10 minutes, or until the mixture is very light and foamy and the whisk leaves a trail that lasts a few seconds when lifted. Sift the flour and carefully fold in with a metal spoon. Fold in the melted white chocolate. Pour the mixture into the prepared pan and bake in a preheated oven at 350°F for 25 minutes, or until springy to the touch. Cool slightly, then transfer to a wire rack to cool completely. Return the cold cake to the pan.

2 To make the truffle topping, place the cream in a pan and bring to a boil, stirring to prevent it from sticking to the bottom of the pan. Allow to cool slightly, then add the white chocolate pieces, and stir until melted and combined. Remove the pan from the heat and stir until almost cool, then stir in the cream cheese. Pour the mixture on top of the cake and chill for about 2 hours. Remove the cake from the pan and transfer to a serving plate.

3 To make large chocolate curls, pour melted chocolate onto a marble or acrylic board and spread it thinly with a spatula. Allow to set at room temperature. Using a peeler, push through the chocolate at a 25 degree angle until a large curl forms. Remove each curl as you make it and refrigerate until set. Decorate the cake with chocolate curls and sprinkle with a little unsweetened cocoa.

Chocolate & Raspberry Vacherin

Serves 10–12

INGREDIENTS

3 egg whites
¾ cup superfine sugar
1 tsp cornstarch
1 ounce dark chocolate, grated

FILLING:
6 ounces dark chocolate
2 cups heavy cream, whipped

2 cups fresh raspberries
a little melted chocolate, to
   decorate

1 Draw three rectangles, 4 x 10 inches, on sheets of baking parchment and place on 2 cookie sheets.

2 Beat the egg whites in a mixing bowl until standing in soft peaks, then gradually beat in half the sugar, and continue beating until the mixture is very stiff and glossy.

3 Carefully fold in the rest of the sugar, the cornstarch, and grated chocolate with a metal spoon or a spatula.

4 Spoon the meringue mixture into a pastry bag fitted with a ½ -inch plain tip, and pipe lines across the rectangles.

5 Bake in a preheated oven at 275°F for 1½ hours, changing the positions of the cookie sheets halfway through. Without opening the oven door, turn off the oven and leave the meringues until they are completely cold, then peel away the paper.

6 To make the filling, melt the chocolate and spread it over 2 of the meringue layers. Leave the filling to harden.

7 Place 1 chocolate-coated meringue on a plate and top with about one-third of the cream and raspberries. Gently place the second chocolate-coated meringue on top and spread with half the remaining cream and raspberries.

8 Place the last meringue on the top and decorate it with the remaining cream and raspberries. Drizzle a little melted chocolate over the top and serve.

Tropical Fruit Vacherin

Serves 10–12

INGREDIENTS

6 egg whites
1¼ cups superfine sugar
¾ cup shredded coconut

FILLING AND TOPPING:
3 ounces dark chocolate, broken
    into pieces
3 egg yolks
3 tbsp water

1 tbsp rum (optional)
4 tbsp superfine sugar
2 cups heavy cream
selection of tropical fruit, sliced or
    cut into bite-size pieces

1 Draw three circles, 8 inches each, on sheets of baking parchment and place them on cookie sheets.

2 Beat the egg whites until standing in soft peaks, then gradually beat in half the sugar and continue beating until the mixture is very stiff and glossy. Carefully fold in the remaining sugar and the coconut.

3 Spoon the mixture into a pastry bag fitted with a star tip and cover the circles with piped swirls. Bake in a preheated oven at 275°F for 1½ hours, changing the position of the cookie sheets halfway through. Without opening the oven door, turn off the oven and leave the meringues until they have cooled completely, then peel away the paper.

4 To make the filling, place the chocolate pieces, egg yolks, water, rum, if using, and sugar in a double boiler over gently simmering water. Cook over a low heat, stirring, until the chocolate has melted and the mixture has thickened. Cover with a disc of baking parchment and set aside until cold.

5 Whip the cream and fold two thirds of it into the chocolate mixture. Sandwich the meringue layers together with the chocolate mixture. Place the remaining cream in a pastry bag fitted with a star tip and pipe around the edge of the meringue. Arrange the tropical fruits in the center.

Olive Oil, Fruit, & Nut Cake

Serves 8

INGREDIENTS

2 cups self-rising flour
4 tbsp superfine sugar
½ cup milk
4 tbsp orange juice

⅔ cup olive oil
⅔ cup mixed dried fruit
¼ cup pine nuts

1 Grease a 7-inch cake pan with a little butter and line with baking parchment.

2 Sift the flour into a large mixing bowl and stir in the superfine sugar.

3 Make a well in the center of the dry ingredients and pour in the milk and orange juice. Stir the mixture with a wooden spoon, beating in the flour and sugar.

4 Pour in the olive oil, and stir so that all the ingredients are well mixed.

5 Stir the mixed dried fruit and pine nuts into the mixture and spoon into the prepared pan.

6 Bake in a preheated oven at 350°F for about 45 minutes, until the cake is golden and firm to the touch.

7 Leave the cake to cool in the pan for a few minutes before transferring to a wire rack to cool further.

8 Serve the cake warm or cold and cut into slices.

COOK'S TIP

Pine nuts are best known as the flavoring ingredient in the classic Italian pesto, but here they give a delicate, slightly resinous flavor to this cake.

Chocolate & Pear Sponge Cake

Serves 6

INGREDIENTS

¾ cup butter, softened

1 cup light brown sugar

3 eggs, beaten

1¼ cups self-rising flour

2 tbsp unsweetened cocoa

2 tbsp milk

2 small pears, peel, cored, and sliced

1 Thoroughly grease an 8-inch loose-bottomed cake pan and line the base with baking parchment.

2 In a bowl, cream together the butter and brown sugar until pale and fluffy.

3 Gradually add the beaten eggs to the creamed mixture, beating well after each addition.

4 Sift the self-rising flour and unsweetened cocoa into the creamed mixture and fold in gently until all of the ingredients are combined.

5 Stir in the milk until well combined, then spoon the mixture into the prepared pan. Level the surface with the back of a spoon or a knife.

6 Place the pear slices on top of the cake mixture, arranging them in a radiating pattern.

7 Bake in a preheated oven at 350°F for about 1 hour, until the cake is just firm to the touch.

8 Let the cake cool in the pan, then transfer to a wire rack until completely cold before serving.

COOK'S TIP

Serve the cake with melted chocolate drizzled over the top for a delicious dessert.

Caraway Madeira Cake

Serves 8

INGREDIENTS

1 cup butter, softened
1 cup light brown sugar
3 eggs, beaten
3 cups self-rising flour

1 tbsp caraway seeds
grated rind of 1 lemon
6 tbsp milk
1 or 2 strips of lemon citron peel

1 Grease and line a 2 pound loaf pan.

2 In a bowl, cream together the butter and brown sugar until pale and fluffy.

3 Gradually add the beaten eggs to the creamed mixture, beating well after each addition.

4 Sift the flour into the bowl and gently fold into the creamed mixture.

5 Add the caraway seeds, lemon rind, and the milk and fold in until thoroughly blended.

6 Spoon the mixture into the prepared pan and level the surface with a knife.

7 Bake in a preheated oven at 325°F for 20 minutes.

8 Remove the cake the oven, place the pieces of lemon peel on top of the cake, and return it to the oven for a further 40 minutes, or until the cake is well risen and a knife inserted into the center comes out clean.

9 Let the cake cool in the pan before turning out and transferring to a wire rack until completely cold.

COOK'S TIP

lemon peel is available in the baking section of supermarkets.
It should be stored in the freezer for maximum freshness.

Clementine Cake

Serves 8

INGREDIENTS

2 clementines

3/4 cup butter, softened

3/4 cup superfine sugar

3 eggs, beaten

1 1/2 cups self-rising flour

3 tbsp ground almonds

3 tbsp light cream

GLAZE AND TOPPING:

6 tbsp clementine juice

2 tbsp superfine sugar

3 white sugar cubes, crushed

1 Thoroughly grease a 7-inch round pan and line the base with baking parchment.

2 Pare the rind from the clementines and chop the rind finely. In a bowl, cream together the butter, sugar, and clementine rind until pale and fluffy.

3 Gradually add the beaten eggs to the mixture, beating well after each addition.

4 Gently fold in the self-rising flour, followed by the ground almonds, and the light cream. Spoon the mixture into the prepared pan.

5 Bake in a preheated oven at 350°F for approximately 55–60 minutes, or until a knife inserted into the center of the cake comes out clean. Cool slightly.

6 To make the glaze. Put the clementine juice into a small pan with the superfine sugar. Bring the mixture to a boil and simmer for 5 minutes.

7 Drizzle the glaze over the cake until it has been absorbed, and sprinkle with the crushed sugar cubes.

COOK'S TIP

If you prefer, chop the rind from the clementines in a food processor or blender together with the sugar in step 2. Tip the mixture into a bowl with the butter and begin to cream the mixture.

Candied Fruit Cake

Serves 8

INGREDIENTS

¾ cup butter, softened
¾ cup superfine sugar
3 eggs, beaten
1½ cups self-rising flour, sifted
3 tbsp ground rice

finely grated rind of 1 lemon
4 tbsp lemon juice
⅔ cup candied fruits, chopped
confectioners' sugar, for dusting
(optional)

1 Lightly grease a 7-inch cake pan with butter and line with baking parchment.

2 In a bowl, whisk together the butter and superfine sugar until light and fluffy.

3 Add the beaten eggs, a little at a time, beating well after each addition. Fold in the flour and ground rice.

4 Add the grated lemon rind and juice, then the chopped candied fruits.

Lightly mix all the ingredients together.

5 Spoon the mixture into the prepared pan and level the surface with the back of a spoon or a knife.

6 Bake in a preheated oven at 350°F for 1–1 hour 10 minutes, until well risen or until a knife inserted into the center of the cake comes out clean.

7 Let the cake cool in the pan for 5 minutes, then turn out onto a wire rack and cool completely.

8 Dust well with a little confectioners' sugar, if using, before serving.

COOK'S TIP

Wash and dry the candied fruits before chopping them. This will prevent the fruits sinking to the bottom of the cake during cooking.

White Chocolate & Apricot Squares

Makes 12 bars

INGREDIENTS

½ cup butter	½ cup superfine sugar	pinch of salt
6 ounces white chocolate, chopped	1¾ cups all-purpose flour, sifted	½ cup chopped ready-to-eat dried
4 eggs	1 tsp baking powder	apricots

1 Lightly grease a 9-inch square cake pan with a little butter or margarine and line the base of the pan with a sheet of baking parchment.

2 Melt the butter and chocolate in a double boiler. Stir until the mixture is smooth and glossy. Let the mixture cool slightly.

3 Beat the eggs and superfine sugar into the butter and chocolate mixture until well combined.

4 Using a metal spoon, fold in the flour, baking powder, salt, and chopped dried apricots and mix all the ingredients together.

5 Pour the mixture into the prepared cake pan and bake in a preheated oven at 350°F for 25–30 minutes.

6 The center of the cake may not be completely firm when it is removed from the oven, but it will set as it cools. Leave in the pan to cool.

7 When the cake is completely cold turn it out and slice into bars or squares.

VARIATION

Replace the white chocolate with milk or dark chocolate, if you prefer.

Crunchy Fruit Cake

Serves 8–10

INGREDIENTS

¹/₃ cup butter, softened
¹/₂ cup superfine sugar
2 eggs, beaten
¹/₃ cup self-rising flour, sifted

²/₃ cup cornmeal
1 tsp baking powder
1²/₃ cups mixed dried fruit
1/4 cup pine nuts

grated rind of 1 lemon
4 tbsp lemon juice
2 tbsp milk

1 Thoroughly grease a 7-inch cake pan and line the base with baking parchment.

2 In a bowl, whisk together the butter and sugar until light and fluffy.

3 Whisk in the beaten eggs, a little at a time, whisking well after each addition.

4 Gently fold the sifted flour, baking powder, and cornmeal into the mixture until thoroughly blended.

5 Stir in the mixed dried fruit, pine nuts, grated lemon rind, lemon juice, and milk.

6 Spoon the mixture into the prepared pan and level the surface.

7 Bake in a preheated oven at 350°F for about 1 hour, or until a knife inserted into the center of the cake comes out clean.

8 Leave the cake to cool in the pan before turning out.

VARIATION

To give a more crumbly light fruit cake, omit the cornmeal and use 1 ¼ cups self-rising flour instead.

Chocolate Slab Cake with Frosting

Serves 10–12

INGREDIENTS

1 cup butter
3 1/2 ounces dark chocolate, chopped
2/3 cup water
2 1/2 cups all-purpose flour

2 tsp baking powder
1 2/3 cups light brown sugar
2/3 cup sour cream
2 eggs, beaten

FROSTING:
7 ounces dark chocolate
6 tbsp water
3 tbsp light cream
1 tbsp butter, chilled

1 Thoroughly grease a 13 × 8-inch square cake pan and line the base with baking parchment. In a saucepan, melt the butter and chocolate, together with the water over a low heat, stirring frequently.

2 Sift the flour and baking powder into a mixing bowl and stir in the sugar.

3 Pour the hot chocolate liquid into the bowl and then beat well until all of the ingredients are evenly mixed. Stir in the sour cream, followed by the eggs.

4 Pour the mixture into the prepared pan and bake in a preheated oven at 375°F for 40–45 minutes.

5 Let the cake cool in the pan before turning it out onto a wire rack. Cool completely.

6 To make the frosting, melt the chocolate with the water in a saucepan over a very low heat, stir in the cream, and remove from the heat. Stir in the chilled butter, then pour the frosting over the cooled cake, using a spatula to spread it evenly over the top of the cake.

Chocolate & Almond Torte

Serves 10

INGREDIENTS

8 ounces dark chocolate,
broken into pieces
3 tbsp water
1 cup light brown sugar
³/₄ cup butter, softened

¹/₄ cup ground almonds
3 tbsp self-rising flour
5 eggs, separated
¹/₄ cup blanched almonds,
finely chopped

confectioners' sugar, for
dusting
heavy cream, to serve
(optional)

1 Grease a 9-inch loose-bottomed cake pan and base line with baking parchment.

2 In a saucepan set over a very low heat, melt the chocolate with the water, stirring until smooth. Add the sugar and stir until dissolved, taking the pan off the heat to prevent it overheating.

3 Add the butter in small amounts until it has melted into the chocolate.

Remove from the heat and lightly stir in the ground almonds and flour. Add the egg yolks, one at a time, beating well after each addition.

4 In a large mixing bowl, whisk the egg whites until they stand in soft peaks, then fold them into the chocolate mixture with a metal spoon. Stir in the chopped almonds. Pour the mixture into the pan and level the surface with the back of a spoon.

5 Bake in a preheated oven at 350°F for 40–45 minutes, until well risen and firm (the cake will crack on the surface during cooking.)

6 Let the cake cool in the pan for 30–40 minutes, then turn it out onto a wire rack to cool completely. Dust with the top with confectioners' sugar, cut the cake in slices, and serve with heavy cream, if using.

Carrot Cake

Makes 12 bars

INGREDIENTS

1 cup self-rising flour
pinch of salt
1 tsp ground cinnamon
¾ cup light brown sugar
2 eggs

scant ½ cup sunflower oil
1 cup finely grated carrot
⅓ cup shredded coconut
⅓ cup walnuts, chopped
walnut pieces, for decoration

FROSTING:
4 tbsp butter, softened
¼ cup full-fat cream cheese
1½ cups confectioners' sugar, sifted
1 tsp lemon juice

1 Lightly grease an 8-inch square cake pan and line with baking parchment.

2 Sift the flour, salt, and ground cinnamon into a large bowl and stir in the brown sugar. Add the eggs and oil to the dry ingredients and mix well.

3 Stir in the grated carrot, shredded coconut, and chopped walnuts.

4 Pour the mixture into the prepared cake pan and bake in a preheated oven at 350°F for 20–25 minutes or until it feels just firm to the touch. Cool in the pan.

5 Meanwhile, make the cheese frosting. In a bowl, beat together the butter, full fat soft cheese, confectioners' sugar, and lemon juice until the mixture is fluffy and creamy.

6 Turn the cake out of the pan and cut into 12 bars or slices. Spread with the frosting and then decorate with walnut pieces.

Lemon Syrup Cake

Serves 8

INGREDIENTS

1¾ cups all-purpose flour	⅔ cup sour cream	SYRUP:
2 tsp baking powder	grated rind 1 large lemon	4 tbsp confectioners' sugar
1 cup superfine sugar	4 tbsp lemon juice	3 tbsp lemon juice
4 eggs	⅔ cup sunflower oil	

1 Lightly grease an 8-inch loose-bottomed round cake pan with butter or margarine and line the base with baking parchment.

2 Sift the flour and baking powder into a bowl and stir in the sugar.

3 In a separate bowl, whisk the eggs, sour cream, lemon rind, lemon juice, and oil together.

4 Pour the egg mixture into the dry ingredients and mix well until evenly combined.

5 Pour the mixture into the prepared pan and bake in a preheated oven at 350°F for about 45–60 minutes, until risen and golden brown.

6 Meanwhile, to make the syrup, mix together the confectioners' sugar and lemon juice in a small saucepan. Stir over a low heat until the mixture starts to bubble and turn syrupy.

7 As soon as the cake comes out of the oven prick the surface with a knife, then brush the syrup over the top. Let the cake cool completely in the pan before turning out and serving.

COOK'S TIP

Pricking the surface of the hot cake ensures that the syrup seeps right into the cake.

Orange Kugelhopf Cake

Serves 6-8

INGREDIENTS

1 cup butter, softened
1 cup superfine sugar
4 eggs, separated
3¾ cups all-purpose flour
3 tsp baking powder

pinch of salt
1¼ cups fresh orange juice
1 tbsp orange flower water
1 tsp grated orange rind

SYRUP:
¾ cup orange juice
1 cup sugar

1 Grease and flour a 10-inch kugelhopf pan or deep ring mold.

2 Cream together the butter and superfine sugar until light and fluffy. Add the egg yolks, one at a time, whisking well after each addition.

3 Sift together the flour, salt, and baking powder. Fold the dry ingredients and the orange juice alternately into the creamed mixture with a metal spoon. Stir in the orange flower water and orange rind.

4 Whisk the egg whites until they reach the soft peak stage and fold them into the mixture.

5 Pour into the prepared mold and bake in a preheated oven at 350°F for 50–55 minutes, or until a knife inserted into center of the cake comes out clean.

6 In a saucepan, bring the orange juice and sugar to a boil, and simmer for 5 minutes until the sugar has dissolved.

7 Remove the cake from the oven and cool in the pan for 10 minutes. Prick the top of the cake with a knife and brush over half of the syrup. Let the cake cool for another 10 minutes. Invert the cake onto a wire rack placed over a deep plate and brush the syrup over the cake until it is entirely covered. Serve.

Coconut Cake

Serves 6-8

INGREDIENTS

2 cups self-rising flour
pinch of salt
½ cup butter, cut into small pieces
½ cup raw crystal sugar

1 cup shredded coconut, plus extra
    for sprinkling
2 eggs, beaten
4 tbsp milk

1 Grease a 2-pound loaf pan and line the base with baking parchment.

2 Sift the flour and salt into a mixing bowl and rub in the butter with your fingertips until the mixture resembles fine breadcrumbs.

3 Stir in the sugar, coconut, eggs, and milk and mix to a soft dropping consistency.

4 Spoon the mixture into the prepared pan and level the surface with the back of a spoon. Bake in a preheated oven at 325°F for 30 minutes.

5 Remove the cake from the oven and sprinkle with the reserved coconut. Return the cake to the oven and cook for another 30 minutes, until well risen with a light golden brown color, and a knife inserted into the center comes out clean.

6 Let the cake cool in the pan before turning out and transferring to a wire rack to cool completely before serving.

COOK'S TIP

The flavor of this cake is enhanced by storing it in a cool dry place for a few days before eating.

Apple Cake with Cider

Makes an 8-inch cake

INGREDIENTS

2 cups self-rising flour

1 tsp baking powder

$\frac{1}{3}$ cup butter, cut into small pieces

$\frac{1}{3}$ cup superfine sugar

$3\frac{1}{2}$ cups chopped dried apple

5 tbsp raisins

$\frac{2}{3}$ cup sweet cider

1 egg, beaten

1 cup raspberries

1 Thoroughly grease an 8-inch cake pan with butter or margarine and line with baking parchment.

2 Sift the flour and baking powder into a bowl and rub in the butter with your fingers until the mixture resembles fine breadcrumbs.

3 Stir in the superfine sugar, chopped dried apple, and the raisins and mix until well combined

4 Pour in the sweet cider and egg and mix together until thoroughly blended. Stir in the raspberries very gently so they do not break up.

5 Pour the mixture into the prepared cake pan.

6 Bake in a preheated oven at 375°F for about 40 minutes, until well risen and a light golden color.

7 Let the cake cool in the pan, then turn out

onto a wire rack. Leave until completely cold before serving. Cut into slices to serve.

VARIATION

If you don't want to use cider, replace it with clear apple juice, if you prefer.

Spiced Apple Ring

Serves 8

INGREDIENTS

³/₄ cup butter, softened
³/₄ cup superfine sugar
3 eggs, beaten

1¹/₂ cups self-rising flour
1 tsp ground cinnamon
1 tsp apple pie spice

2 eating apples, cored and grated
2 tbsp apple juice or milk
¹/₄ cup slivered almonds

---

1 Lightly grease a 10-inch ovenproof ring mold.

2 In a mixing bowl, cream together the butter and sugar until light and fluffy. Gradually add the beaten eggs, beating well after each addition, until well combined.

3 Sift the flour and spices, then carefully fold them into the creamed mixture.

4 Stir in the grated apples and the apple juice or milk and mix together to form a soft dropping consistency.

5 Sprinkle the slivered almonds around the base of the mold and spoon the cake mixture on top. Level the surface with the back of the spoon.

6 Bake in a preheated oven at 350°F for about 30 minutes, until well risen and a knife inserted into the center comes out clean.

7 Let the cake cool in the pan for about 10 minutes before turning out and transferring to a wire rack to cool completely. Serve the spiced apple ring cut into slices.

COOK'S TIP

This cake can also be made in a 7-inch round cake pan if you do not have an ovenproof ring mold.

Marbled Chocolate Cake

Serves 8

INGREDIENTS

¾ cup butter, softened

¾ cup superfine sugar

3 eggs, beaten

1¼ cups self-rising flour, sifted

¼ cup unsweetened cocoa, sifted

5–6 tbsp orange juice

grated rind of 1 orange

1 Lightly grease a 10-inch ovenproof ring mold.

2 In a mixing bowl, cream together the butter and sugar with an electric mixer for about 5 minutes.

3 Add the beaten egg, a little at a time, beating well after each addition.

4 Using a metal spoon, carefully fold the flour into the creamed mixture. Spoon half of the mixture into a separate mixing bowl.

5 Fold the cocoa and half of the orange juice into one bowl and mix gently.

6 Fold the orange rind and remaining orange juice into the other bowl and mix gently.

7 Place spoonfuls of each of the mixtures alternately into the mold, then drag a knife through the mixture to create a marbled effect.

8 Bake in a preheated oven at 350°F for 30–35 minutes, until well risen and a knife inserted into the center comes out clean.

9 Let the cake cool in the mold before turning out onto a wire rack. Serve the cake cut into slices.

VARIATION

For a richer chocolate flavor, add ⅓ cup chocolate chips to the cocoa mixture.

Coffee & Almond Streusel Cake

Serves 8

INGREDIENTS

1¼ cups all-purpose flour
1 tbsp baking powder
⅓ cup superfine sugar
⅔ cup milk
2 eggs

½ cup butter, melted and cooled
2 tbsp instant coffee mixed with
   1 tbsp boiling water
⅓ cup almonds, chopped
confectioners' sugar, for dusting

TOPPING:
½ cup self-rising flour
⅓ cup raw crystal sugar
2 tbsp butter, cut into
   small pieces
1 tsp apple pie spice
1 tbsp water

1 Thoroughly grease a 9-inch loose-bottomed round cake pan and line with baking parchment. Sift together the flour and baking powder into a large mixing bowl, then stir in the superfine sugar.

2 Whisk the milk, eggs, butter, and coffee mixture together and pour onto the dry ingredients. Add the chopped almonds and mix lightly together. Spoon the mixture into the pan.

3 To make the topping, mix the flour and raw crystal sugar together in a separate bowl. Rub in the butter with your fingers until the mixture is crumbly. Sprinkle in the apple pie spice and the water and bring the mixture together in loose crumbs.

Sprinkle the topping over the cake mixture.

4 Bake in a preheated oven at 375°F for 50 minutes–1 hour. Cover loosely with foil if the topping starts to brown too quickly. Let the cake cool in the pan, then turn out to cool completely. Dust with a little confectioners' sugar just before serving.

Sugar-Free Fruit Cake

Serves 8–10

INGREDIENTS

3 cups all-purpose flour
2 tsp baking powder
1 tsp apple pie spice
1/2 cup butter, cut into small pieces
3/4 cup chopped ready-to-eat
    dried apricots
1/2 cup pitted chopped dates

1/2 cup candied cherries, chopped
2/3 cup raisins
1/2 cup milk
2 eggs, beaten
grated rind of 1 orange
5–6 tbsp orange juice
3 tbsp clear honey

1 Grease an 8-inch round cake pan and line the base with baking parchment.

2 Sift the flour, baking powder, and apple pie spice into a large mixing bowl.

3 Rub in the butter with your fingers until the mixture resembles fine breadcrumbs.

4 Carefully stir in the chopped apricots, dates, candied cherries, and raisins with the milk, beaten eggs, grated orange rind, and orange juice and mix well together.

5 Stir in the honey and mix everything together to a soft dropping consistency. Spoon the mixture into the prepared cake pan and level the surface.

6 Bake in a preheated oven at 350°F for 1 hour until a knife inserted into the center of the cake comes out clean.

7 Let the cake cool in the pan before turning out.

VARIATION

For a fruity alternative, replace the honey with 1 mashed ripe banana, if you prefer.

Almond Cake

Serves 8

INGREDIENTS

$\frac{1}{3}$ cup soft margarine
3 tbsp light brown sugar
2 eggs
1$\frac{1}{2}$ cups self-rising flour

1 tsp baking powder
4 tbsp milk
2 tbsp clear honey
$\frac{1}{2}$ cup slivered almonds

SYRUP:
$\frac{2}{3}$ cup clear honey
2 tbsp lemon juice

1 Thoroughly grease a 7-inch round cake pan and line with baking parchment.

2 Place the margarine, brown sugar, eggs, flour, baking powder, milk, and honey in a large mixing bowl and beat well with a wooden spoon for about 1 minute, until all of the ingredients are thoroughly mixed together.

3 Spoon into the prepared pan, level the surface, and sprinkle with the almonds.

4 Bake the mixture in a preheated oven at 350°F for 50 minutes, or until the cake is well risen.

5 To make the syrup, combine the honey and lemon juice in a small pan and simmer for 5 minutes, or until the syrup starts to coat the back of a spoon.

6 As soon as the cake comes out of the oven, pour the syrup on top, allowing it to seep into the middle of the cake.

7 Let the cake cool for at least 2 hours before slicing.

Gingerbread

Makes 12 bars

INGREDIENTS

²/₃ cup butter
1 cup light brown sugar
2 tbsp molasses
2 cups all-purpose flour

1 tsp baking powder
2 tsp baking soda
2 tsp ground ginger
²/₃ cup milk

1 egg, beaten
2 eating apples, peeled, chopped,
    and coated with 1 tbsp lemon
    juice

1 Thoroughly grease a 9-inch square cake pan with butter or margarine and line with baking parchment.

2 Melt the butter, sugar, and molasses in a saucepan over a low heat and let the mixture cool.

3 Sift the flour, baking powder, soda, and ginger into a mixing bowl.

4 Stir in the milk, beaten egg, and cooled butter, sugar, and molasses mixture, followed by the chopped apples coated with the lemon juice.

5 Mix everything together gently, then pour the mixture into the prepared pan.

6 Bake in a preheated oven at 325°F for 30–35 minutes, until the cake has risen and a knife inserted into the center comes out clean.

7 Let the cake cool in the pan before turning out onto a wire rack and cutting into 12 bars.

VARIATION

If you enjoy the flavor of ginger, try adding 2 tablespoons finely chopped preserved ginger to the mixture in step 3.

Pear & Ginger Cake

Serves 4–6

INGREDIENTS

⁷/₈ cup sweet butter, softened
³/₄ cup superfine sugar
1¹/₂ cups self-rising flour, sifted

3 tsp ground ginger
1 pound eating pears, peeled, cored,
and thinly sliced

3 eggs, beaten
1 tbsp brown sugar
ice cream or heavy cream to serve

1 Lightly grease and line the base of a deep 8-inch cake pan.

2 Using a whisk, combine ³/₄ cup of the butter with the superfine sugar, flour, ginger, and eggs and mix to form a smooth consistency.

3 Spoon the cake mixture into the prepared pan, leveling the surface.

4 Arrange the pear slices over the cake mixture. Sprinkle with the brown sugar and dot with the remaining butter.

5 Bake in a preheated oven at 350°F for 35–40 minutes, or until the cake is golden and feels springy to the touch.

6 Serve the pear and ginger cake warm, with ice cream or cream, if desired.

COOK'S TIP

To test whether the cake is cooked through, insert a knife into the center of the cake. If it comes out clean the cake is cooked through.

COOK'S TIP

Brown sugar is often known as Barbados sugar. It is a darker form of light-brown sugar.

Eggless Sponge Cake

Makes one 8-inch cake

INGREDIENTS

1¾ cups self-rising whole-
　wheat flour
2 tsp baking powder
¾ cup superfine sugar
6 tbsp sunflower oil

1 cup water
1 tsp vanilla extract
4 tbsp strawberry or raspberry
　reduced-sugar spread
superfine sugar, for dusting

1 Thoroughly grease two 8-inch layer pans with butter and line them with baking parchment.

2 Sift the flour and baking powder into a large mixing bowl, stirring in any bran remaining in the strainer. Stir in the superfine sugar.

3 Pour in the oil, water, and vanilla extract and mix together with a wooden spoon for about 1 minute until the cake mixture is a smooth consistency.

4 Divide the mixture between the prepared pans, levelling the surface with the back of a spoon.

5 Bake in a preheated oven at 350°F for 25–30 minutes, until the center springs back when lightly touched. Leave to cool in the pans before turning out and transferring to a wire rack.

6 To serve the cake, remove the baking parchment and place one of the sponges onto a serving plate. Cover with the strawberry or raspberry spread and place the other sponge on top. Dust with a little superfine sugar and cut into slices.

VARIATION

Use melted vegan butter or margarine instead of the sunflower oil if you prefer, but allow it to cool before adding it to the dry ingredients in step 3.

Small Cakes & Cookies

This chapter contains everyday delights for baking fans. You are sure to be tempted by our wonderful array of cookies and small cakes. Make any day special with a home-made cookie to be served with coffee, as a snack, or to accompany a special dessert. Although some take a little longer to make, most are quick and easy to prepare, and decoration is often simple, although you can get carried away if you like!

You'll find recipes for old favorites and some new cookies and small cakes to tickle your taste-buds. Finally, we have given the chocolate treatment to some traditional recipes, turning them into chocoholic delights.

Chocolate Boxes

Makes 4

INGREDIENTS

8 ounces dark chocolate

8 ounces bought or ready-made
    plain or chocolate cake

2 tbsp apricot preserve

²/₃ cup heavy cream

1 tbsp maple syrup

prepared fresh fruit, such as small
    strawberries, raspberries, kiwi
    fruit, or red currants

1 Melt the dark chocolate and spread it evenly over a large sheet of baking parchment. Allow to harden in a cool room.

2 When just set, cut the chocolate into 2-inch squares and remove from the paper. Make sure that your hands are as cool as possible and handle the chocolate as little as possible.

3 Cut the cake into two 2-inch cubes, then cut each cube in half. Warm the apricot preserve

and brush it over the sides of the cake cubes. Carefully press a chocolate square onto each side of the cake cubes to make 4 chocolate boxes with cake at the bottom. Chill for 20 minutes.

4 Whip the heavy cream with the maple syrup until just holding its shape. Spoon or pipe a little of the mixture into each chocolate box.

5 Decorate the top of each box with the prepared fruit. If desired, the fruit can be partially

dipped into melted chocolate and allowed to harden before putting into the boxes.

COOK'S TIP

For the best results, keep the boxes well chilled and fill and decorate them just before you want to serve them.

Chocolate Cream Wraps

Makes 6–8

INGREDIENTS

2 eggs
4 tbsp superfine sugar

⅓ cup all-purpose flour
1½ tbsp unsweetened cocoa

4 tbsp apricot preserve
⅔ cup heavy cream, whipped
confectioners' sugar, to dust

1 Line 2 cookie sheets with pieces of baking parchment. Beat the eggs and sugar together until the mixture is very light and fluffy and the whisk leaves a trail when lifted.

2 Sift together the flour and unsweetened cocoa. Using a metal spoon or a spatula, gently fold it into the eggs and sugar in a figure eight movement.

3 Drop rounded tablespoons of the mixture onto the lined cookie sheets and spread them into oval shapes. Make sure they are well spaced, as they will spread during cooking.

4 Bake in a preheated oven at 425°F for about 6–8 minutes, or until springy to the touch. Leave the cakes on the cookie sheets to cool.

5 When cold, slide the cakes onto a damp dish cloth and set aside until cold. Carefully remove them from the dampened cloth. Spread the flat side of the cakes with apricot preserve, then spoon or pipe the whipped cream down the center of each one.

6 Fold the cakes in half and place them on a serving plate. Sprinkle them with a little confectioners' sugar and serve.

VARIATION

Fold 4 tsp of crème de menthe or 2 ounces melted chocolate into the cream for fabulous alternatives to plain cream wraps.

Chocolate Cupcakes with White Chocolate Frosting

Makes 18

INGREDIENTS

½ cup butter, softened
7 tbsp superfine sugar
2 eggs, lightly beaten
2 tbsp milk

⅓ cup dark chocolate chips
1¼ cups self-rising flour
¼ cup unsweetened cocoa

FROSTING:
8 ounces white chocolate
5½ ounces low-fat cream cheese

1 Line an 18-hole muffin pan with individual paper cups.

2 Beat together the butter and sugar until pale and fluffy. Gradually add the eggs, beating well after each addition. Add a little of the flour if the mixture begins to curdle. Add the milk, then fold in the chocolate chips.

3 Sift together the flour and unsweetened cocoa and fold into the mixture with a metal spoon or spatula. Divide the mixture equally between the paper cups and level the tops.

4 Bake in a preheated oven at 350°F for 20 minutes, or until well risen and springy to the touch. Transfer the cupcakes to a wire rack to cool.

5 To make the frosting, melt the chocolate, then let cool slightly. Beat the cream cheese until softened and beat in the chocolate. Spread a little frosting over each cake and chill for 1 hour.

VARIATION

Add white chocolate chips or chopped pecans to the mixture instead of the dark chocolate chips, if you wish. You can also add the finely grated rind of 1 orange for a chocolate and orange flavor.

Chocolate Rum Babas

Makes 4

INGREDIENTS

³/₄ cup strong all-purpose flour
¹/₄ cup unsweetened cocoa
1 envelope active dry yeast
pinch of salt
1 tbsp superfine sugar
1¹/₂ ounces dark chocolate, grated
2 eggs

3 tbsp tepid milk
4 tbsp butter, melted

SYRUP:
4 tbsp clear honey
2 tbsp water
4 tbsp rum

TO SERVE:
whipped cream
unsweetened cocoa, to dust
fresh fruit (optional)

1 Lightly oil 4 individual ring pans. In a large warmed mixing bowl, sift the flour and unsweetened cocoa together. Stir in the yeast, salt, sugar, and grated chocolate. Beat the eggs, add the milk and butter, and beat until well mixed.

2 Make a well in the center of the dry ingredients and pour in the egg mixture, beating to mix to a batter. Beat for 10 minutes, ideally with an electric mixer with a dough hook. Divide the mixture between the pans – it should come halfway up the sides.

3 Place on a cookie sheet and cover with a damp dish cloth. Leave in a warm place until the mixture rises almost to the tops of the pans. Bake in a preheated oven at 400°F for 15 minutes.

4 To make the syrup, gently heat all the ingredients in a small pan. Turn out the babas and place on a rack placed above a tray to catch the syrup.

Drizzle the syrup over the babas and leave for at least 2 hours for the syrup to soak in. Once or twice, spoon the syrup that has dripped onto the tray over the babas.

5 Fill the center of the babas with whipped cream and sprinkle a little unsweetened cocoa over the top. Serve the babas with fresh fruit, if desired.

No-Bake Chocolate Squares

Makes 16

INGREDIENTS

9 1/2 ounces dark chocolate
3/4 cup butter
4 tbsp light corn syrup
2 tbsp dark rum (optional)

6 ounces plain cookies
1/3 cup toasted rice cereal
1/2 cup chopped walnuts or
pecan nuts

1/2 cup candied cherries,
roughly chopped
1 ounce white chocolate,
to decorate

1 Place the dark chocolate in a double boiler with the butter, syrup, and rum, if using, over gently simmering water until melted, stirring continuously until blended.

2 Break the cookies into small pieces and stir into the chocolate mixture, along with the rice cereal, nuts, and cherries.

3 Line a 7-inch square cake pan with baking parchment. Pour the mixture into the pan and level the top, pressing down well with the back of a spoon. Chill in the refrigerator for 2 hours.

4 To decorate, melt the white chocolate and drizzle it over the top of the cake in a random pattern. Let set. To serve, carefully turn out of the pan and remove the baking parchment. Cut the cake into 16 squares.

COOK'S TIP

Store in an airtight container in the refrigerator for up to 2 weeks.

VARIATIONS

For a coconut flavor, replace the rice cereal with shredded coconut and add a coconut-flavored liqueur.

VARIATIONS

Brandy or an orange-flavored liqueur can be used instead of the rum, if you wish. Cherry brandy also works well.

Chocolate Butterfly Cupcakes

Makes 12

INGREDIENTS

$^1/_2$ cup soft margarine
$^1/_2$ cup superfine sugar
2 large eggs
$1^1/_4$ cups self-rising flour
2 tbsp unsweetened cocoa
1 ounce dark chocolate, melted

LEMON BUTTER CREAM:
$^1/_2$ cup sweet butter, softened
$1^1/_3$ cups confectioners' sugar, sifted
grated rind of $^1/_2$ lemon
1 tbsp lemon juice
confectioners' sugar, to dust

1 Place 12 paper cups in a muffin pan. Place all the ingredients for the cakes, except the melted chocolate, in a large mixing bowl and beat with an electric mixer until the mixture is just smooth. Beat in the chocolate.

2 Spoon equal amounts of the cake mixture into each paper cup, filling them three-quarters full. Bake in a preheated oven at 350°F for 15 minutes, or until springy to the touch. Transfer the cakes to a wire rack and set aside to cool completely.

3 To make the lemon butter cream, place the butter in a mixing bowl and beat until fluffy, then gradually beat in the confectioners' sugar.

VARIATION

For a chocolate butter cream, beat the butter and confectioners' sugar together, then beat in 1 ounce melted dark chocolate.

Beat in the lemon rind and gradually add the lemon juice, beating well.

4 When cold, cut the top off each cupcake, using a serrated knife. Cut each top in half.

5 Spread or pipe the butter cream frosting over the cut surface of each cake and push the 2 cut pieces of cake top into the frosting to form wings. Sprinkle with confectioners' sugar.

Sticky Chocolate Brownies

Makes 9

INGREDIENTS

$^1/_2$ cup sweet butter

$^3/_4$ cup superfine sugar

$^1/_2$ cup dark brown sugar

$4^1/_2$ ounces dark chocolate

1 tbsp light corn syrup

2 eggs

1 tsp chocolate or vanilla extract

$^3/_4$ cup all-purpose flour

2 tbsp unsweetened cocoa

$^1/_2$ tsp baking powder

1 Lightly grease and flour a shallow 8-inch square cake pan.

2 Place the butter, sugars, dark chocolate, and light corn syrup in a heavy-based saucepan and heat gently, stirring until the mixture is well blended and smooth. Remove from the heat and let cool.

3 Beat together the eggs and extract. Beat in the cooled chocolate mixture.

4 Sift together the flour, unsweetened cocoa, and baking powder and fold carefully into the egg and chocolate mixture, using a metal spoon or a spatula.

5 Spoon the mixture into the prepared pan and bake in a preheated oven at 350°F for 25 minutes, until the top is crisp and the edge of the cake is beginning to shrink away from the pan. The inside of the cake will still be quite dense and soft to the touch.

6 Allow the cake to cool completely in the pan, then cut it into squares to serve.

VARIATION

This cake can be well wrapped and frozen for up to 2 months. Thaw at room temperature for about 2 hours or overnight in the refrigerator.

Chocolate Fudge Brownies

Makes 16

INGREDIENTS

7 ounces low-fat cream cheese	¹/₂ cup butter	FUDGE FROSTING:
¹/₂ tsp vanilla extract	3 tbsp unsweetened cocoa	2 tbsp butter
2 eggs	³/₄ cup self-rising flour, sifted	1 tbsp milk
1¹/₄ cups superfine sugar	1³/₄ ounces pecans, chopped	¹/₂ cup confectioners' sugar
		2 tbsp unsweetened cocoa
		pecans, to decorate (optional)

1 Lightly grease and flour a shallow 8-inch square cake pan.

2 Beat together the cheese, vanilla extract, and 5 tsp of the superfine sugar until smooth, then set aside.

3 Beat the eggs and remaining superfine sugar together until light and fluffy. Place the butter and unsweetened cocoa in a small saucepan and heat gently, stirring until the butter melts and the mixture combines, then stir it into the egg mixture. Fold in the flour and the chopped pecans, mixing well.

4 Pour half the brownie mixture into the pan and level the surface. Carefully spread the soft cheese over it, then cover it with the remaining brownie mixture. Bake in a preheated oven at 350°F for 40–45 minutes. Cool in the pan.

5 To make the frosting, melt the butter in the milk. Stir in the confectioners' sugar and unsweetened cocoa. Spread the frosting over the brownies and decorate with pecans, if using. Let the frosting set, then cut the brownies into squares to serve.

VARIATION

Omit the cheese layer if preferred. Use walnuts in place of pecans.

Chocolate Chip Muffins

Makes 12

INGREDIENTS

1/2 cup soft margarine	2 large eggs	2 cups all-purpose flour
1 cup superfine sugar	2/3 cup full-fat unsweetened yogurt	1 tsp baking soda
	5 tbsp milk	6 ounces dark chocolate chips

1 Line a muffin pan with 12 paper cups.

2 Place the margarine and sugar in a large mixing bowl and beat with a wooden spoon until light and fluffy. Beat in the eggs, yogurt, and milk until combined.

3 Sift the flour and baking soda together and add to the mixture. Stir until just blended.

4 Stir in the chocolate chips, then spoon the mixture into the paper cups, and bake in a preheated oven at 375°F for 25 minutes, or until a toothpick inserted into the center comes out clean. Cool the muffins in the pan for 5 minutes, then turn them out onto a wire rack to cool completely.

VARIATION

For chocolate and orange muffins, add the grated rind of 1 orange and replace the milk with fresh orange juice.

VARIATION

The mixture can also be used to make 6 large or 24 mini muffins. Bake mini muffins for 10 minutes, or until springy to the touch.

Chocolate Biscuits

Makes 9

INGREDIENTS

2 cups self-rising flour, sifted
1/4 cup butter
1 tbsp superfine sugar

1/3 cup chocolate chips
about 2/3 cup milk

1 Lightly grease a cookie sheet. Place the flour in a mixing bowl. Cut the butter into small pieces and rub it into the flour with your fingertips until the biscuit mixture resembles fine bread crumbs.

2 Stir in the superfine sugar and chocolate chips.

3 Mix in enough milk to form a soft dough.

4 On a lightly floured surface, roll out the dough to form a rectangle 4 x 6 inches, about 1 inch thick. Cut the dough into 9 squares.

5 Place the biscuits on the prepared cookie sheet, spacing them well apart.

6 Brush with a little milk and bake in a preheated oven at 425°F for 10–12 minutes, until the biscuits are risen and golden. Let cool slightly and serve warm.

COOK'S TIP

To be at their best, all biscuits should be freshly baked and served warm. Split the warm biscuits and spread them with a little chocolate and hazelnut spread or a spoon of whipped cream.

VARIATION

Use dark, milk, or white chocolate chips or a mixture of all three. Use a 2-inch cookie cutter to cut out round biscuits, if preferred.

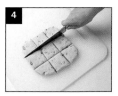

Pain au Chocolate

Makes 12

INGREDIENTS

4 cups strong all-purpose flour
$^1/_2$ tsp salt
1 envelope active dry yeast
2 tbsp white vegetable shortening

1 egg, beaten lightly
1 cup tepid water
$^3/_4$ cup butter, softened

$3^1/_2$ ounces dark chocolate, broken
    into 12 squares
beaten egg, to glaze
confectioners' sugar, to dust

1 Lightly grease a cookie sheet. Sift the flour and salt into a mixing bowl and stir in the yeast. Rub in the shortening with your fingertips. Add the egg and enough of the water to mix to a soft dough. Knead it for about 10 minutes to make a smooth elastic dough.

2 Roll out to form a rectangle 15 x 8 inches. Divide the butter into 3 portions and dot one portion over two-thirds of the rectangle, leaving a small border around the edge.

3 Fold the rectangle into 3 by first folding the plain part of the dough over and then the other side. Seal the edges of the dough by pressing with a rolling pin. Give the dough a quarter turn so the sealed edges are at the top and bottom. Re-roll and fold (without adding butter), then wrap the dough, and chill for 30 minutes.

4 Repeat steps 2 and 3 until all the butter has been used, chilling the dough each time. Re-roll and fold twice more without butter. Chill for a final 30 minutes.

5 Roll the dough to a rectangle 18 x 12 inches, trim and cut in half lengthwise. Cut each half into 6 rectangles and brush with beaten egg. Place a chocolate square at one end of each rectangle and roll up to form a sausage. Press the ends together and place, seam side down, on the cookie sheet. Cover and set aside to rise for 40 minutes in a warm place. Brush with beaten egg to glaze and bake in a preheated oven at 425°F for 20–25 minutes, until golden. Cool on a wire rack. Serve warm or cold.

Choc-Chip Tartlets

Makes 6

INGREDIENTS

1½ cups toasted hazelnuts	FILLING:	3 tbsp chocolate and hazelnut
1¾ cups all-purpose flour	2 tbsp cornstarch	spread
1 tbsp confectioners' sugar	1 tbsp unsweetened cocoa	2½ tbsp dark chocolate chips
⅓ cup soft margarine	1 tbsp superfine sugar	2½ tbsp milk chocolate chips
	1¼ cups low-fat milk	2½ tbsp white chocolate chips

1 Finely chop the nuts in a food processor. Add the flour, sugar, and margarine. Process for a few seconds, until the mixture resembles breadcrumbs. Add 2–3 tbsp water and process to form a soft dough. Cover and chill in the freezer for 10 minutes.

2 Roll out the dough and use it to line six 4-inch tartlet pans. Prick the bases with a fork and line them with loosely crumpled foil. Bake in a preheated oven at 400°F for 15 minutes.

Remove and discard the foil and bake for a further 5 minutes, until the pie shells are crisp and golden. Remove from the oven and set aside to cool.

3 Mix together the cornstarch, unsweetened cocoa, and sugar with enough milk to make a smooth paste. Stir in the remaining milk. Pour into a pan and cook gently over a low heat, stirring until thickened and smooth. Stir in the chocolate and hazelnut spread.

4 Mix together the chocolate chips and reserve a quarter. Stir half the remaining chips into the custard. Cover with damp wax paper and leave until almost cold, then stir in the second half of the chocolate chips. Spoon the mixture into the pie shells and set aside to cool. Decorate with the reserved chips, scattering them over the top.

Chocolate Eclairs

Makes about 10

INGREDIENTS

CHOUX PASTRY:
$^2/_3$ cup water
$^1/_4$ cup butter, cut into small pieces
$^3/_4$ cup strong all-purpose
    flour, sifted
2 eggs

PATISSERIE CREAM:
2 eggs, lightly beaten
4 tbsp superfine sugar
2 tbsp cornstarch
$1^1/_4$ cups milk
$^1/_4$ tsp vanilla extract

FROSTING:
2 tbsp butter
1 tbsp milk
1 tbsp unsweetened cocoa
$^1/_2$ cup confectioners' sugar
a little white chocolate, melted

1 Lightly grease a cookie sheet. Place the water in a saucepan, add the butter, and heat gently until the butter melts. Bring to a rolling boil, then remove the pan from the heat, and add the flour all at once, beating constantly until the mixture leaves the sides of the pan and forms a ball. Let cool slightly, then gradually beat in the eggs to form a smooth, glossy mixture. Spoon the mixture into a large pastry bag fitted with a $^1/_2$-inch plain tip.

2 Sprinkle the cookie sheet with a little water. Pipe éclairs 3 inches long, spaced well apart. Bake in a preheated oven at 400°F for 30–35 minutes, or until crisp and golden. Make a small slit in each one to let the steam escape. Cool on a rack.

3 To make the patisserie cream, beat the eggs and sugar until thick and creamy, then fold in the cornstarch. Heat the milk until almost boiling and pour into the eggs, beating constantly.

Transfer to the pan and cook over a low heat, stirring until thick. Remove the pan from the heat and stir in the vanilla extract. Cover with baking parchment and cool. To make the frosting, melt the butter with the milk in a pan, remove from the heat, and stir in the cocoa and sugar. Split the éclairs lengthwise and pipe in the patisserie cream. Spread the frosting over the top of the éclairs. Spoon the white chocolate on top, swirl it in, and let set.

Chocolate Meringues

Makes 8

INGREDIENTS

4 egg whites
1 cup superfine sugar
1 tsp cornstarch
1½ ounces dark chocolate, grated

TO COMPLETE:
3½ ounces dark chocolate
⅔ cup heavy cream

1 tbsp confectioners' sugar
1 tbsp brandy (optional)

1 Line 2 cookie sheets with baking parchment. Beat the egg whites until they are standing in soft peaks, then gradually beat in half the superfine sugar. Continue beating until the mixture is very stiff and glossy.

2 Carefully fold in the remaining sugar, the cornstarch, and grated chocolate with a metal spoon or spatula.

3 Spoon the mixture into a pastry bag fitted with a large star or plain tip. Pipe 16 large rosettes or mounds on the lined cookie sheets.

4 Bake in a preheated oven at 275°F for about 1 hour, changing the position of the cookie sheets halfway through cooking. Without opening the oven door, turn off the oven, and leave the meringues to cool in the oven. Once cold, carefully peel away the baking parchment.

5 Melt the dark chocolate and spread it over the base of the meringues. Stand them upside down on a wire rack until the chocolate has set. Whip the heavy cream together with confectioners' sugar and brandy (if using), until the cream holds its shape. Spoon into a pastry bag and use to sandwich the meringues together in pairs. Serve.

VARIATION

To make mini meringues, use a star shaped tip and pipe about 24 small rosettes. Bake for about 40 minutes, until crisp.

Chocolate & Hazelnut Palmiers

Makes about 26

INGREDIENTS

13 ounces ready-made puff
pastry dough

8 tbsp chocolate hazelnut spread
$^1/_2$ cup chopped toasted hazelnuts

5 tsp superfine sugar

1 Lightly grease a cookie sheet. On a lightly floured surface, roll out the puff pastry dough to a rectangle about 15 x 9 inches in size.

2 Spread the chocolate hazelnut spread over the dough using a spatula, then scatter the chopped hazelnuts over the top.

3 Roll up one long side of the dough to the center, then roll up the other side so that they meet in the center. Where the pieces meet, dampen the edges with a little water to join them. Using a sharp knife, cut into thin slices.

Place each slice onto the prepared cookie sheet and flatten slightly with a spatula. Sprinkle the slices with the superfine sugar.

4 Bake in a preheated oven at 425°F, for about 10–15 minutes, until golden. Transfer to a wire rack to cool.

COOK'S TIP

Palmiers can be served cold, but they are also delicious served warm.

The cookies can be frozen for up to 3 months in a sealed container.

VARIATION

For an extra chocolate flavour, dip the palmiers in melted dark chocolate to half-cover each biscuit.

Chocolate & Coconut Squares

Makes 9

INGREDIENTS

8 ounces dark chocolate
    graham crackers
1/3 cup butter or margarine
6 ounce can evaporated milk

1 egg, beaten
1 tsp vanilla extract
5 tsp superfine sugar
1/3 cup self-rising flour, sifted

1 1/4 cups shredded coconut
1 3/4 ounces dark chocolate
    (optional)

1 Grease a shallow 8-inch square cake pan and line the base with baking parchment.

2 Put the crackers in a plastic bag and crush them with a rolling pin or process them in a food processor.

3 Melt the butter or margarine in a saucepan and stir in the crushed crackers until well combined.

4 Press the mixture into the base of the cake pan.

5 Beat together the evaporated milk, egg, vanilla extract, and sugar until smooth. Stir in the flour and shredded coconut. Pour the mixture over the cracker base and level the top.

6 Bake in a preheated oven at 375°F for 30 minutes, or until the coconut topping is firm and just golden.

7 Cool in the cake pan for about 5 minutes, then cut into squares. Allow to cool completely in the pan.

8 Carefully remove the squares from the pan and place them on a board. Melt the dark chocolate (if using) and drizzle it over the squares to decorate them. Let the chocolate set before serving.

COOK'S TIP

Store the squares in an airtight container for up to 4 days. They can be frozen, undecorated, for up to 2 months. Thaw at room temperature.

Chocolate & Coconut Cookies

Makes about 24

INGREDIENTS

$^1/_3$ cup soft margarine

1 tsp vanilla extract

6 tbsp confectioners' sugar, sifted

1 cup all-purpose flour

2 tbsp unsweetened cocoa

$^2/_3$ cup shredded coconut

2 tbsp butter

$3^1/_2$ ounces white marshmallows

$^1/_4$ cup shredded coconut

a little dark chocolate, melted

1 Lightly grease a cookie sheet. Beat together the margarine, vanilla extract, and confectioners' sugar in a mixing bowl until light and fluffy. Sift together the flour and unsweetened cocoa and beat into the mixture, together with the coconut.

2 Roll heaping teaspoons of the mixture into balls between your palms and place on the prepared cookie sheet, allowing room for the cookies to spread during cooking.

3 Flatten the balls slightly and bake in a preheated oven at 350°F for 12–15 minutes, until the cookies are just firm.

4 Leave the cookies to cool on the cookie sheet for a few minutes before transferring to a wire rack to cool completely.

5 Combine the butter and marshmallows in a small saucepan and heat gently, stirring until melted and well combined. Spread a little of the frosting mixture over each cookie and dip in the coconut. Let set. Decorate the cookies with a little melted chocolate and let set completely before serving.

COOK'S TIP

Store these cookies in an airtight container for about 1 week. Alternatively, they can be frozen, undecorated, for up to 2 months.

Chocolate Crispy Bites

Makes 16

INGREDIENTS

WHITE LAYER:
4 tbsp butter
1 tbsp light corn syrup
5 1/2 ounces white chocolate
1/2 cup toasted rice cereal

DARK LAYER:
4 tbsp butter
2 tbsp light corn syrup

4 1/2 ounces dark chocolate, broken
into small pieces
3/4 cup toasted rice cereal

1 Lightly grease an 8-inch square cake pan and line with baking parchment.

2 To make the white chocolate layer, melt the butter, light corn syrup, and chocolate in a double boiler.

3 Remove from the heat and stir in the rice cereal until it is well combined.

4 Press into the prepared pan and level the surface of the mixture.

5 To make the dark chocolate layer, melt the butter, light corn syrup, and dark chocolate in a double boiler.

6 Remove from the heat and stir in the rice cereal until it is well coated. Pour the dark chocolate layer over the hardened white chocolate layer and refrigerate until the top layer has hardened.

7 Turn out of the cake pan and cut into small, evenly sized squares, using a sharp knife.

COOK'S TIP

These bites can be made up to 4 days ahead. Keep them covered in the refrigerator until ready to use.

Dutch Macaroons

Makes about 20

INGREDIENTS

rice paper
2 egg whites

1 cup superfine sugar
1½ cups ground almonds

8 ounces dark chocolate

1 Cover 2 cookie sheets with rice paper. Beat the egg whites in a large mixing bowl until stiff, then fold in the sugar and ground almonds.

2 Place the mixture in a large pastry bag fitted with a ½-inch plain tip and pipe fingers, about 3 inches long, allowing space for the mixture to spread during cooking.

3 Bake in a preheated oven at 350°F for 15–20 minutes, until golden. Transfer to a wire rack and let cool. Remove the excess rice paper from around the edges of the cookies.

4 Melt the chocolate and dip the base of each cookie into the chocolate. Place the macaroons on a sheet of baking parchment and allow to set.

5 Drizzle any remaining chocolate over the top of the cookies. Set completely before serving.

COOK'S TIP

Rice paper is edible so you can break off the excess from around the edge of the cookies. Remove it completely before dipping in the chocolate, if you prefer.

VARIATION

Almonds are most commonly used in macaroons, but they can be made with other ground nuts, such as hazelnuts.

Chocolate Orange Cookies

Makes about 30

INGREDIENTS

⅓ cup butter, softened
⅓ cup superfine sugar
1 egg

1 tbsp milk
2 cups all-purpose flour
¼ cup unsweetened cocoa

FROSTING:
1 cup confectioners' sugar, sifted
3 tbsp orange juice
a little dark chocolate, melted

1 Line 2 cookie sheets with baking parchment.

2 Beat together the butter and sugar until light and fluffy. Beat the egg and milk into the mixture until well combined. Sift together the flour and unsweetened cocoa and gradually mix together to form a soft dough. Use your fingers to incorporate the last of the flour and bring the dough together.

3 Roll out the dough on a lightly floured surface until ¼-inch thick. Using a 2-inch fluted round cutter, cut out as many cookies as you can. Re-roll the dough trimmings and cut out more cookies.

4 Place the cookies on the prepared cookie sheet, spaced apart, and bake in a preheated oven at 350°F for 10–12 minutes, or until golden.

5 Cool the cookies on the cookie sheet for a few minutes, then transfer to a wire rack to cool completely.

6 To make the frosting, place the confectioners' sugar in a bowl and stir in enough orange juice to form a thin frosting that will coat the back of a spoon. Spread the frosting over the cookies and let set. Drizzle with melted chocolate. Allow the chocolate to set before serving.

Chocolate Caramel Squares

Makes 16

INGREDIENTS

¹/₃ cup soft margarine
4 tbsp light brown sugar
1 cup all-purpose flour
¹/₂ cup rolled oats

CARAMEL FILLING:
2 tbsp butter
2 tbsp light brown sugar
7 ounce can condensed milk

TOPPING:
3¹/₂ ounces dark chocolate
1 ounce white chocolate (optional)

1 Beat together the margarine and brown sugar in a bowl until light and fluffy. Beat in the flour and the rolled oats. Use your fingertips to bring the mixture together, if necessary.

2 Press the mixture into the base of a shallow 8-inch square cake pan.

3 Bake in a preheated oven at 350°F for about 25 minutes, or until just golden and firm. Cool in the pan.

4 Place the ingredients for the caramel filling in a pan and heat gently, stirring until the sugar has dissolved and the ingredients combine. Bring to a boil over a very low heat, then boil very gently for 3-4 minutes, stirring constantly until thickened.

5 Pour the caramel filling over the cookie base in the pan and let set.

6 Melt the dark chocolate and spread it over the caramel. If using the white chocolate, melt it and pipe lines of white chocolate over the dark chocolate. Using a toothpick, feather the white chocolate into the dark chocolate. Let set completely. Cut into squares to serve.

COOK'S TIP

If desired, you can line the pan with baking parchment so that the cookie can be lifted out before cutting into pieces.

Chocolate Chip Oatmeal Bars

Makes 12

INGREDIENTS

$^1/_2$ cup butter

$^1/_3$ cup superfine sugar

1 tbsp light corn syrup

4 cups rolled oats

$^1/_2$ cup dark chocolate chips

$^1/_3$ cup golden raisins

1 Lightly grease a shallow 8-inch square cake pan.

2 Place the butter, superfine sugar, and light corn syrup in a saucepan and cook over a low heat, stirring constantly, until the butter and sugar have melted and the mixture is well combined.

3 Remove the pan from the heat and stir in the rolled oats with a wooden spoon until they are well coated. Add the chocolate chips and the golden raisins and mix well to combine all the ingredients thoroughly.

4 Turn into the prepared pan and press down well.

5 Bake in a preheated oven at 350°F for 30 minutes. Cool slightly, then mark into bars or squares. When almost cold cut into bars or squares and transfer to a wire rack until cold.

COOK'S TIP

The bars will keep in an airtight container for up to 1 week, but they are so delicious they are unlikely to last that long!

VARIATION

Replace some of the oats with chopped nuts or sunflower seeds and a littleextra dried fruit. extra dried fruit.

Chocolate Chip Cookies

Makes about 18

INGREDIENTS

1/2 cup soft margarine	1/2 tsp vanilla extract	1 tsp baking powder
1/3 cup light brown sugar	1 egg	2/3 cup dark chocolate chips
1/4 cup superfine sugar	1 1/2 cups all-purpose flour	

1 Lightly grease 2 cookie sheets.

2 Place all of the ingredients in a large mixing bowl in the order listed and beat until well combined.

3 Place tablespoonfuls of the mixture onto the prepared cookie sheets, spacing them well apart to allow for spreading during cooking.

4 Bake in a preheated oven at 375°F for 10–12 minutes, or until the cookies are golden brown.

5 Using a spatula, transfer the cookies to a wire rack to cool completely.

VARIATIONS

For Choc & Nut Cookies, add 1/2 cup chopped hazelnuts to the basic mixture.

For Double Choc Cookies, beat in 1 1/2 ounces melted dark chocolate.

VARIATIONS

For White Chocolate Chip Cookies, use white chocolate chips instead of the dark chocolate chips.

For Mixed Chocolate Chip Cookies, use a mixture of dark, milk, and white chocolate chips in the basic mixture.

For Chocolate Chip & Coconut Cookies, add 1/3 cup shredded coconut to the basic mixture.

For Chocolate Chip & Raisin Cookies, add 5 tbsp raisins to the basic mixture.

Chocolate Shortbread

Makes 12

INGREDIENTS

4 tbsp superfine sugar
2/3 cup butter, softened

1 1/2 cups all-purpose flour
1 tbsp unsweetened cocoa

1 3/4 ounces dark chocolate,
finely chopped

1 Lightly grease
a cookie sheet.

2 Place all the
ingredients in a large
mixing bowl in the order
listed and beat together
until they form a dough.
Knead the dough lightly.

3 Place the dough on
the cookie sheet and
roll or press out to form
an 8-inch round.

4 Pinch the edges of
the dough with your
fingertips to form a
decorative edge. Prick the
dough all over with a fork
and mark into 12 wedges,
using a sharp knife.

5 Bake in a preheated
oven at 325°F for
40 minutes, until firm
and golden. Cool slightly
before cutting into wedges.
Transfer to a wire rack to
cool completely.

VARIATION

*The shortbread dough
can be pressed into
a floured shortbread
mold and turned out
onto the cookie sheet
before baking.*

VARIATION

*For round shortbread
cookies, roll out the
dough on a lightly floured
surface to 1/3 inch thick.
Cut out 3-inch rounds
with a cookie cutter.
Transfer to a greased
cookie sheet and bake
as above. If desired,
coat half the cookie
in melted chocolate.*

Malted Chocolate Wedges

Makes 16

INGREDIENTS

7 tbsp butter

2 tbsp light corn syrup

2 tbsp malted chocolate drink

8 ounces malted milk cookies

2¾ ounces milk or dark chocolate, broken into pieces

2 tbsp confectioners' sugar

2 tbsp milk

1 Grease a shallow 7-inch round cake pan or flan pan and line the base.

2 Place the butter, light corn syrup, and malted chocolate drink in a small pan and heat gently, stirring all the time until the butter has melted and the mixture is well combined.

3 Crush the cookies in a plastic bag with a rolling pin, or process them in a food processor until they form crumbs. Stir the crumbs into the chocolate mixture and mix well.

4 Press the mixture into the prepared pan and chill in the refrigerator until firm.

5 Heat the chocolate pieces in a double boiler with the confectioners' sugar and the milk. Stir until the chocolate melts and the mixture is thoroughly combined.

6 Spread the chocolate frosting over the cookie base and allow to set in the pan. Using a sharp knife, cut into wedges to serve.

VARIATION

Add chopped pecan nuts to the cookie crumb mixture in step 3, if desired.

Chocolate Checkerboard Cookies

Makes about 18

INGREDIENTS

³/₄ cup butter, softened
6 tbsp confectioners' sugar

1 teaspoon vanilla extract or grated
    rind of ¹/₂ orange
2¹/₄ cups all-purpose flour

1 ounce dark chocolate, melted
a little beaten egg white

1 Lightly grease a cookie sheet. Beat the butter and confectioners' sugar in a mixing bowl until light and fluffy. Beat in the vanilla extract or the grated orange rind.

2 Gradually beat in the flour to form a soft dough. Use your fingers to incorporate the last of the flour and to bring the dough together.

3 Divide the dough into 2 equal pieces and beat the melted chocolate into one half. Keeping each half of the dough separate, cover and chill in the refrigerator for about 30 minutes.

4 Roll out each piece of dough to a rectangle about 3 x 8 inches long and 1¹/₂ inches thick. Brush one piece of dough with a little egg white and place the other piece of dough on top.

5 Cut the block of dough in half lengthwise and turn over one half. Brush the side of one strip with egg white and butt the other up to it, so that it resembles a checkerboard.

6 Cut the block into thin slices and place each slice flat on the cookie sheet, allowing enough room for them to spread a little during cooking.

7 Bake in a preheated oven at 350°F for about 10 minutes, until just firm. Cool on the cookie sheets for a few minutes before carefully transferring to a wire rack with a spatula. Cool completely.

Viennese Chocolate Fingers

Makes about 18

INGREDIENTS

½ cup sweet butter

6 tbsp confectioners' sugar

1½ cups self-rising flour, sifted

3 tbsp cornstarch

7 ounces dark chocolate

1 Lightly grease 2 cookie sheets. Beat the butter and sugar together in a mixing bowl until light and fluffy. Gradually beat the flour and cornstarch into the mixture.

2 Melt 2¾ ounces of the dark chocolate and beat into the cookie dough.

3 Place in a pastry bag fitted with a large star tip and pipe fingers about 2 inches long on the prepared cookie sheets, slightly spaced apart to allow for spreading during cooking.

4 Bake in a preheated oven at 375°F for 12–15 minutes. Cool slightly on the cookie sheets, then carefully transfer with a spatula to a wire rack and let cool completely.

5 Melt the remaining dark chocolate and dip one end of each cookie in the chocolate, allowing the excess to drip back into the bowl.

6 Place the cookies on a sheet of baking parchment and allow to completely set before serving.

COOK'S TIP

If the cookie dough is too thick to pipe, beat in a little milk to thin it out.

VARIATION

Dip the base of each cookie in melted chocolate and allow to set. Sandwich the cookies together in pairs with a little butter cream.

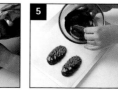

Chocolate Pretzels

Makes about 30

INGREDIENTS

1/2 cup sweet butter
7 tbsp superfine sugar
1 egg
2 cups all-purpose flour
1/4 cup unsweetened cocoa

TO FINISH:
1 tbsp butter
3 1/2 ounces dark chocolate
confectioners' sugar, to dust

1 Lightly grease a cookie sheet. Beat together the butter and sugar in a mixing bowl until light and fluffy. Beat in the egg.

2 Sift together the flour and unsweetened cocoa and gradually beat in to form a soft dough. Use your fingers to incorporate the last of the flour and bring the dough together. Chill for 15 minutes.

3 Break small pieces from the dough and roll them into thin sausage shapes about 4 inches long and 1/4-inch thick. Twist into pretzel shapes by first making a circle and then twisting the ends through each other to form a letter "B."

4 Place the pretzels on the prepared cookie sheet, slightly spaced apart to allow room for spreading during cooking.

5 Bake in a preheated oven at 375°F for 8–12 minutes. Allow the pretzels to cool slightly on the cookie sheet, then transfer to a wire rack to cool completely.

6 Melt the butter and chocolate in a double boiler, stirring to combine.

7 Dip half of each pretzel into the chocolate and allow the excess chocolate to drip back into the bowl. Place the pretzels on a sheet of baking parchment and allow to set.

8 When set, dust the non-chocolate coated side of each pretzel with confectioners' sugar before serving.

Chocolate Wheat Cookies

Makes about 20

INGREDIENTS

¹/₃ cup butter

7 tbsp raw crystal sugar

1 egg

1 ounce wheatgerm

1 cup whole-wheat self-rising flour

¹/₂ cup self-rising flour, sifted

4¹/₂ ounces chocolate

1 Lightly grease a cookie sheet. Beat the butter and sugar until fluffy. Add the egg and beat well. Stir in the wheatgerm and flours. Bring the mixture together with your hands.

2 Roll heaping teaspoons of the mixture into balls and place on the prepared cookie sheet, allowing room for the cookies to spread during cooking.

3 Flatten the cookies slightly with a fork. Bake in a preheated oven at 350°F for 15–20 minutes, until golden. Cool on the cookie sheet for a few minutes before transferring the cookies to a wire rack to cool completely.

4 Melt the chocolate, then dip each cookie in the chocolate to cover the base and come a little way up the sides. Let the excess drip back into the bowl.

5 Place the cookies, chocolate side up, on a sheet of baking parchment and allow to set in a cool place before serving.

COOK'S TIP

These cookies can be frozen very successfully. Freeze them at the end of step 3 for up to 3 months. Thaw and then dip them in melted chocolate.

Apricot Slices

Makes 12

INGREDIENTS

PIE DOUGH:

1³/4 cups whole-wheat flour
¹/2 cup finely ground mixed nuts
¹/3 cup vegan margarine, cut into
    small pieces

4 tbsp water
soy milk, to glaze

FILLING:

2 cups dried apricots
grated rind of 1 orange
1¹/3 cups apple juice
1 tsp ground cinnamon
¹/3 cup raisins

1 Lightly grease a 9-inch square cake pan. To make the pie dough, place the flour and nuts in a mixing bowl and rub in the margarine with your fingers until the mixture resembles breadcrumbs. Stir in the water and form a dough. Wrap and chill for 30 minutes.

2 To make the filling, place the apricots, orange rind, and apple juice in a saucepan and bring to a boil. Simmer for 30 minutes, until the apricots are mushy. Cool slightly, then blend to a purée. Stir in the ground cinnamon and raisins.

3 Divide the pie dough in half, roll out one half, and use to line the base of the pan. Spread the apricot purée over the top and brush the edges of the pie dough with water. Roll out the rest of the dough to fit over the top of the apricot purée. Press down, sealing the edges with a teaspoon.

4 Prick the top of the pie dough with a fork and brush with a little soy milk. Bake in a preheated oven at 400°F for 20–25 minutes, until the pastry is a golden color. Cool slightly before cutting into 12 bars. Serve warm or cold.

Apple Shortcakes

Serves 8

INGREDIENTS

1¼ cups all-purpose flour	FILLING:	⅔ cup heavy cream, whipped
½ tsp salt	3 eating apples, peeled, cored,	lightly
1 tsp baking powder	and sliced	confectioners' sugar, for dusting
1 tbsp superfine sugar	½ cup superfine sugar	
1 tbsp butter, cut into	1 tbsp lemon juice	
small pieces	1 tsp ground cinnamon	
¼ cup milk	1⅓ cups water	

1 Lightly grease a cookie sheet.

2 Sift together the flour, salt, and baking powder into a mixing bowl. Stir in the sugar, then rub in the butter until the mixture resembles fine breadcrumbs. Pour in the milk and mix everything to a soft dough.

3 Knead the dough lightly, then roll out to a thickness of ½ inch. Stamp out 4 rounds, using a 2-inch cutter. Transfer the rounds to the prepared cookie sheet. Bake in a preheated oven at 425°F for about 15 minutes, until the shortcakes are well risen and lightly browned. Let the shortcakes cool.

4 To make the filling, place the apple slices, sugar, lemon juice, and cinnamon in a saucepan. Add the water, bring to a boil, and simmer uncovered for 5–10 minutes, until the apples are tender. Cool a little, then remove the apples from the pan.

5 To serve, split the shortcakes in half. Place each bottom half on an individual serving plate and spoon on a quarter of the apple slices, then the cream. Place the other half of the shortcake on top. Serve dusted with confectioners' sugar, if desired.

Rich Biscuits

Makes 8

| INGREDIENTS |

2 cups self-rising flour	$^1/_3$ cup butter, cut into small pieces	1 egg, beaten
1 tbsp superfine sugar	1 eating apple, peeled, cored,	2 tbsp molasses
pinch of salt	and chopped	5 tbsp milk

1 Lightly grease a cookie sheet.

2 Sift the flour, sugar, and salt into a mixing bowl.

3 Rub in the butter with your fingers until the mixture resembles fine breadcrumbs.

4 Stir the chopped apple into the mixture until combined.

5 Mix the beaten egg, molasses, and milk together. Add to the dry ingredients to form a soft dough.

6 On a lightly floured kitchen counter, roll out the dough to a thickness of $^3/_4$ inch and cut out 8 scones, using a 2-inch plain pastry cutter.

7 Arrange the scones on the prepared cookie sheet and bake in a preheated oven at 425°F for 8–10 minutes.

8 Transfer the scones to a wire rack and cool slightly before serving.

9 Serve split in half and spread with butter.

COOK'S TIP

These scones can be frozen, but are best defrosted and eaten within 1 month.

Cherry Biscuits

Makes 8

INGREDIENTS

2 cups self-rising flour	$^1/_3$ cup butter, cut into small pieces	1 egg, beaten
1 tbsp superfine sugar	3 tbsp candied cherries, chopped	$^1/_4$ cup milk
pinch of salt	3 tbsp golden raisins	

1 Lightly grease a cookie sheet with a little butter.

2 Sift together the flour, sugar, and salt into a mixing bowl and rub in the butter with your fingers until the scone mixture resembles breadcrumbs.

3 Stir in the candied cherries and golden raisins. Add the beaten egg.

4 Reserve 1 tablespoon of the milk for glazing, then add the remainder to the mixture. Mix together to form a soft dough.

5 On a lightly floured surface, roll out the dough to a thickness of $^3/_4$ inch and cut out 8 scones, using a 2-inch plain pastry cutter.

6 Place the scones on the cookie sheet and brush with the reserved milk.

7 Bake in a preheated oven at 425°F for 8–10 minutes, or until the scones are golden brown.

8 Let cool slightly on a wire rack, then serve split and buttered.

COOK'S TIP

These scones will freeze very successfully, but they are best defrosted and eaten within 1 month.

Cranberry Muffins

Makes 18

INGREDIENTS

2 cups all-purpose flour

2 tsp baking powder

1/2 tsp salt

3 tbsp superfine sugar

4 tbsp butter, melted

2 eggs, beaten

3/4 cup milk

1 cup fresh cranberries

2 tbsp freshly grated Parmesan cheese

1 Lightly grease 2 muffin pans with a little butter

2 Sift the flour, baking powder, and salt into a mixing bowl. Stir in the superfine sugar.

3 In a separate bowl, mix the butter, beaten eggs, and milk together, then pour into the bowl of dry ingredients.

4 Mix lightly together until all of the ingredients are evenly combined, then stir in the fresh cranberries.

5 Divide the mixture between the prepared pans.

6 Sprinkle the grated Parmesan cheese over the top of each muffin mixture.

7 Bake in a preheated oven at 400°F for about 20 minutes, or until the cranberry muffins are well risen and a golden brown color.

8 Let the muffins cool slightly in the pans. Transfer the muffins to a wire rack and cool completely before serving.

VARIATION

For a sweet alternative to this recipe, replace the Parmesan cheese with raw crystal sugar in step 5, if you prefer.

Spiced Cookies

Makes about 24

INGREDIENTS

³/₄ cup sweet butter
1 cup dark brown sugar
2 cups all-purpose flour
pinch of salt

¹/₂ tsp baking soda
1 tsp ground cinnamon
¹/₂ tsp ground coriander

¹/₂ tsp ground nutmeg
¹/₄ tsp ground cloves
2 tbsp dark rum

1 Lightly grease 2 cookie sheets with a little butter.

2 In a large mixing bowl, cream together the butter and dark brown sugar and beat until light and fluffy.

3 Sift the flour, salt, baking soda, cinnamon, coriander, nutmeg, and cloves into the creamed mixture and mix well until all the ingredients are thoroughly combined.

4 Stir the dark rum into the creamed mixture.

5 Using 2 teaspoons, place small mounds of the mixture onto the cookie sheets 3 inches apart to allow for spreading during cooking. Flatten each mound slightly with the back of a spoon.

6 Bake in a preheated oven at 350°F for about 10 minutes, or until golden.

7 Transfer the cookies to wire racks and let them cool and crispen before serving.

COOK'S TIP

Use the back of a fork to flatten the cookies slightly before baking.

Cinnamon & Sunflower Squares

Makes 12

INGREDIENTS

1 cup butter, softened
1¼ cups superfine sugar
3 eggs, beaten

2 cups self-rising flour
½ tsp baking soda
1 tbsp ground cinnamon

⅔ cup sour cream
⅔ cup sunflower seeds

1 Grease a 9-inch square cake pan with a little butter and line the base with baking parchment.

2 Put the butter and superfine sugar into a large mixing bowl and cream them together until the mixture becomes light and fluffy.

3 Gradually add the beaten eggs to the mixture, beating well after each addition.

4 Sift the flour, baking soda, and ground cinnamon into the creamed mixture and fold in gently, using a metal spoon.

5 Spoon in the sour cream and sunflower seeds and gently mix together until well combined.

6 Spoon the mixture into the prepared cake pan and level the surface with the back of a spoon or a knife.

7 Bake in a preheated oven at 350°F for about 45 minutes, or until the mixture is firm to the touch when pressed.

8 Loosen the edges with a round-bladed knife, then turn out onto a wire rack to cool completely. Slice into 12 squares and serve.

COOK'S TIP

These moist squares will freeze well and keep for up to 1 month.

Gingernuts

Makes 30

INGREDIENTS

3 cups self-rising flour

pinch of salt

1 cup superfine sugar

1 tbsp ground ginger

1 tsp baking soda

$^1/_2$ cup butter

$^1/_4$ cup light corn syrup

1 egg, beaten

1 tsp grated orange rind

1 Lightly grease several cookie sheets with butter or margarine.

2 Sift the flour, salt, sugar, ginger, and baking soda into a large mixing bowl.

3 Heat the butter and light corn syrup together in a saucepan over a very low heat until the butter has completely melted.

4 Let the butter mixture cool slightly, then pour it onto the dry ingredients.

5 Add the egg and orange rind and mix thoroughly.

6 Using your hands, carefully shape the dough into 30 even-size balls.

7 Place the balls on the prepared cookie sheets, spacing them well apart to allow for spreading during cooking, then flatten them slightly with your fingers.

8 Bake in a preheated oven at 325°F for 15–20 minutes, then transfer

the gingernuts to a wire rack to cool before serving.

VARIATION

If you like your gingernuts crunchy, bake them in the oven for a few minutes longer.

Caraway Cookies

Makes about 36

INGREDIENTS

2 cups all-purpose flour

pinch of salt

^{1}/₃ cup butter, cut into small pieces

1^1/₄ cups superfine sugar

1 egg, beaten

2 tbsp caraway seeds

raw crystal sugar, for sprinkling

(optional)

1 Lightly grease several cookie sheets with butter.

2 Sift the flour and salt into a mixing bowl. Rub in the butter with your fingertips until the mixture resembles fine breadcrumbs. Stir in the superfine sugar.

3 Reserve 1 tablespoon of the beaten egg for brushing the cookies and add the rest to the mixture, together with the caraway seeds. Bring together to form a soft dough.

4 On a lightly floured surface, roll out the cookie dough thinly and then cut out about 36 rounds with a 2^1/₂-inch cookie cutter.

5 Transfer the cookies to the prepared cookie sheets, brush with the reserved beaten egg, and sprinkle with a little raw crystal sugar.

6 Bake in a preheated oven at 325°F for 10–15 minutes, until the ccokies are crisp and lightly golden in color.

7 Let the cookies cool on a wire rack and store in an airtight container.

VARIATION

Caraway seeds have a nutty, delicate anise flavor. If you don't like their flavor, replace the caraway seeds with the milder-flavored poppy seeds.

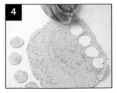

Peanut Butter Cookies

Makes 20

INGREDIENTS

½ cup butter, softened
½ cup chunky peanut butter
1 cup sugar

1 egg, lightly beaten
1¼ cups all-purpose flour
½ tsp baking powder

pinch of salt
¾ cup unsalted natural peanuts,
    chopped

1 Lightly grease
2 cookie sheets.

2 In a large mixing bowl,
beat together the butter
and peanut butter.

3 Gradually add the sugar
and beat well.

4 Add the beaten egg,
a little at a time,
beating until it is
thoroughly combined.

5 Sift the flour, baking
powder, and salt into
the peanut butter mixture.

6 Add the peanuts
and bring all of
the ingredients together
to form a soft dough.
Wrap and chill for about
30 minutes.

7 Form the dough into
20 balls and place them
onto the prepared cookie
sheets about 2 inches apart to
allow for spreading. Flatten
them slightly with a fork.

8 Bake in a preheated
oven at 375°F for
15 minutes, until a golden
brown color. Transfer

the cookies to a wire rack
and cool slightly before
serving.

COOK'S TIP

*For a crunchy
bite and sparkling
appearance, sprinkle the
cookies with raw crystal
sugar just before they
are baked.*

Hazelnut Squares

Makes 16

INGREDIENTS

1¼ cups all-purpose flour
pinch of salt
1 tsp baking powder

⅓ cup butter, cut into small pieces
1 cup light brown sugar
1 egg, beaten

4 tbsp milk
1 cup hazelnuts, halved
raw crystal sugar, for sprinkling
(optional)

1 Grease a 9-inch square cake pan and line the base with baking parchment.

2 Sift the flour, salt, and baking powder into a large mixing bowl.

3 Rub in the butter with your fingers until the mixture resembles fine breadcrumbs. Stir in the brown sugar.

4 Add the egg, milk, and nuts to the mixture and stir well until all the ingredients are thoroughly combined.

5 Spoon the mixture into the prepared cake pan and level the surface. Sprinkle with raw crystal sugar, if using.

6 Bake in a preheated oven at 350°F for about 25 minutes, or until firm to the touch.

7 Cool slightly for 10 minutes, loosen the edges with a round-bladed knife, and turn out onto a wire rack to cool further. Cut into squares.

VARIATION

For a coffee-time cookie, replace the milk with the same amount of cold strong black coffee—the stronger the better!

Coconut Cookies

Makes 16 squares

INGREDIENTS

1 cup butter
1⅓ cups raw crystal sugar

2 tbsp light corn syrup
3½ cups dried oats

1 cup shredded coconut
⅓ cup candied cherries, chopped

1 Lightly grease a 12 × 9-inch cookie sheet with butter.

2 Heat the butter, raw crystal sugar, and light corn syrup in a large saucepan over a low heat until just melted.

3 Stir in the oats, shredded coconut, and candied cherries and mix well until all the ingredients are combined.

4 Spread the mixture onto the cookie sheet and press down with the back of a spatula to make a smooth surface.

5 Bake in a preheated oven at 325°F for about 30 minutes.

6 Remove the cookies from the oven and let them cool slightly on the cookie sheet for about 10 minutes.

7 Cut the mixture into even-sized rectangles using a sharp knife.

8 Carefully transfer the coconut cookies to a wire rack and cool completely.

COOK'S TIP

These cookies are best stored in an airtight container and eaten within 1 week. They can also be frozen for up to 1 month.

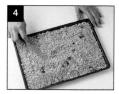

Oat & Raisin Cookies

Makes 10

INGREDIENTS

4 tbsp butter	$^1/_2$ cup all-purpose flour	2 cups oats
$^1/_2$ cup superfine sugar	$^1/_2$ tsp salt	$^3/_4$ cup raisins
1 egg, beaten	$^1/_2$ tsp baking powder	2 tbsp sesame seeds

1 Lightly grease 2 cookie sheets.

2 In a large mixing bowl, cream together the butter and sugar until light and fluffy.

3 Add the beaten egg gradually and beat until well combined.

4 Sift the flour, salt and baking powder into the creamed mixture. Mix well.

5 Add the oats, raisins, and sesame seeds and mix together thoroughly.

6 Place spoonfuls of the mixture well apart (to allow for spreading during baking) on the prepared cookie sheets and flatten them slightly with the back of a spoon.

7 Bake the cookies in a preheated oven at 350°F for 15 minutes.

8 Let the cookies cool slightly on the cookie sheets.

9 Transfer the cookies to a wire rack and cool completely before serving.

VARIATION

Substitute chopped ready-to-eat dried apricots for the raisins, if you prefer.

COOK'S TIP

To enjoy these cookies at their best, store them in an airtight container.

Rosemary Cookies

Makes about 25

INGREDIENTS

2 tbsp butter, softened
4 tbsp superfine sugar
grated rind of 1 lemon

4 tbsp lemon juice
1 egg, separated
2 tsp finely chopped fresh rosemary

1¾ cups all-purpose flour, sifted
superfine sugar, for sprinkling
(optional)

1 Lightly grease 2 cookie sheets with butter or margarine.

2 In a large mixing bowl, cream together the butter and sugar until pale and fluffy.

3 Add the lemon rind and juice, then the egg yolk, and beat until all the ingredients are thoroughly combined. Stir in the chopped fresh rosemary.

4 Add the sifted flour, mixing well until a soft dough is formed.

Wrap and chill in the refrigerator for 30 minutes.

5 On a lightly floured surface, roll out the dough thinly and stamp out about 25 cookies with a 2½-inch cookie cutter. Arrange the dough on the prepared cookie sheets.

6 In a small bowl, lightly beat the egg white. Gently brush the egg white over the surface of each cookie, then sprinkle with a little superfine sugar, if desired.

7 Bake the cookies in a preheated oven at 350°F for about 15 minutes.

8 Transfer the cookies to a wire rack and cool completely before serving.

VARIATION

In place of the fresh rosemary, use 1½ teaspoons of dried rosemary, if you prefer.

Citrus Crescents

Makes about 25

INGREDIENTS

⅓ cup butter, softened
⅓ cup superfine sugar
1 egg, separated

1¾ cups all-purpose flour
grated rind of 1 orange
grated rind of 1 lemon

grated rind of 1 lime
2–3 tbsp orange juice
superfine sugar, for sprinkling
(optional)

1 Lightly grease 2 cookie sheets.

2 In a mixing bowl, cream together the butter and sugar until light and fluffy, then gradually pour in the egg yolk, beating well after each addition.

3 Sift the flour into the creamed mixture and mix until evenly combined. Add the orange, lemon, and lime rinds to the mixture with enough of the orange juice to make a soft dough.

4 Roll out the dough on a lightly floured surface. Stamp out cookies using a 3-inch cookie cutter. Make crescent shapes by cutting away a quarter of each cookie. Re-roll the pastry trimmings to make about 25 crescents.

5 Prick the surface of each crescent with a fork. Place the crescents onto the cookie sheets.

6 Lightly beat the egg white in a small bowl and gently brush it over the cookies.

Dust the cookies with extra superfine sugar, if using.

7 Bake in a preheated oven at 400°F for 12–15 minutes. Transfer the cookies to a wire rack and cool slightly before serving.

COOK'S TIP

Store the citrus crescents in an airtight container or freeze them for up to 1 month.

Lemon Jumbles

Makes about 50

INGREDIENTS

⅓ cup butter, softened
½ cup superfine sugar
grated rind of 1 lemon

1 egg, beaten
4 tbsp lemon juice
3 cups all-purpose flour

1 tsp baking powder
1 tbsp milk
confectioners' sugar, for dredging

1 Lightly grease several cookie sheets with butter.

2 In a mixing bowl, cream together the butter, superfine sugar, and lemon rind until pale and fluffy.

3 Add the beaten egg and lemon juice a little at a time, beating well after each addition.

4 Sift the flour and baking powder into the creamed mixture and blend together until well combined.

Add the milk, mixing to form a dough.

5 Turn the dough out onto a lightly floured surface and divide into about 50 equal-size pieces.

6 Roll each piece into a sausage shape with your hands and twist in the middle to make an "S" shape.

7 Place the shapes on the cookie sheets and bake in a preheated oven at 325°F for 15–20 minutes. Cool completely on a wire rack and dredge with confectioners' sugar before serving.

VARIATION

If you prefer, shape the dough into other shapes—letters of the alphabet or geometric shapes—or just make into round cookies.

Chocolate & Lemon Pinwheels

Makes about 40

INGREDIENTS

³/₄ cup butter, softened
1¹/₃ cups superfine sugar

1 egg, beaten
3 cups all-purpose flour

1 ounce dark chocolate, melted and
cooled slightly
grated rind of 1 lemon

1 Grease and flour several cookie sheets.

2 In a large mixing bowl, cream together the butter and sugar until light and fluffy.

3 Gradually add the beaten egg to the creamed mixture, beating well after each addition.

4 Sift the flour into the creamed mixture and mix until a soft dough forms.

5 Transfer half of the dough to another bowl and beat in the cooled melted chocolate.

6 Stir the grated lemon rind into the other half of the plain dough.

7 On a lightly floured surface, roll out the 2 pieces of dough to form rectangles of the same size.

8 Lay the lemon dough on top of the chocolate dough. Roll up the dough tightly into a sausage shape, using a sheet of baking parchment to guide you. Let the dough chill slightly in the refrigerator.

9 Cut the roll into about 40 slices, place them on the cookie sheets, and bake in a preheated oven at 375°F for 10–12 minutes, or until lightly golden. Transfer the pinwheels to a wire rack and cool completely before serving.

White Chocolate Cookies

Makes 24

$\frac{1}{2}$ cup butter, softened
$\frac{3}{4}$ cup light brown sugar
1 egg, beaten

$1\frac{3}{4}$ cups self-rising flour
pinch of salt

$4\frac{1}{2}$ ounces white chocolate,
    roughly chopped
$\frac{1}{2}$ cup chopped Brazil nuts

1 Lightly grease several cookie sheets.

2 In a large mixing bowl, cream together the butter and sugar until light and fluffy.

3 Gradually add the beaten egg to the creamed mixture, beating well after each addition.

4 Sift the flour and salt into the creamed mixture and blend well.

5 Stir in the chocolate chunks and Brazil nuts.

6 Place heaping teaspoons of the white chocolate mixture onto the prepared cookie sheets. Space them well apart as the cookies will spread considerably during cooking.

7 Bake in a preheated oven at 375°F for 10–12 minutes, or until the cookies are a light golden brown color.

8 Transfer the cookies to wire racks and set aside until completely cold and crisp before serving.

VARIATION

Use dark or milk chocolate instead of white chocolate, if you prefer.

Shortbread Fantails

Makes 8

INGREDIENTS

¹/₂ cup butter, softened
¹/₄ cup sugar
¹/₄ cup confectioners' sugar

2 cups all-purpose flour
pinch of salt
2 tsp orange flower water

superfine sugar, for sprinkling

1 Lightly grease an 8-inch shallow round cake pan with a little butter.

2 In a large mixing bowl, cream together the butter, the sugar, and the confectioners' sugar until the mixture is light and fluffy.

3 Sift the flour and salt into the creamed mixture. Add the orange flower water and bring everything together to form a soft dough.

4 On a lightly floured surface, roll out the dough to an 8-inch round and place in the pan. Prick the dough well and score into 8 triangles with a round-bladed knife.

5 Bake in a preheated oven at 300°F for 30–35 minutes, or until the cookie is crisp and pale golden in color.

6 Sprinkle with a little superfine sugar, then cut along the marked lines to make the fantails.

7 Let the shortbread cool completely before removing the pieces from the pan. Store in an airtight container.

COOK'S TIP

For a crunchy addition, sprinkle 2 tablespoons of chopped mixed nuts over the top of the fantails before baking.

Millionaire's Shortbread

Makes 12 bars

INGREDIENTS

1 1/2 cups all-purpose flour
1/2 cup butter, cut into small pieces
3 tbsp light brown sugar, sifted

TOPPING:
4 tbsp butter
3 tbsp light brown sugar

14 ounce can condensed milk
5 1/2 ounces milk chocolate

1 Thoroughly grease a 9-inch square cake pan.

2 Sift the flour into a bowl and rub in the butter with your fingertips until the mixture resembles fine breadcrumbs. Add the sugar and mix to form a firm dough.

3 Press the dough into the prepared pan and prick with a fork.

4 Bake in a preheated oven at 375°F for 20 minutes, until lightly golden. Cool completely in the pan.

5 To make the topping, place the butter, sugar, and condensed milk in a nonstick saucepan and cook over a gentle heat, stirring constantly, until the mixture comes to a boil.

6 Reduce the heat and cook for 4–5 minutes, until the caramel is pale golden and thick and is coming away from the sides of the pan. Pour over the shortbread base and let cool.

7 When the caramel topping is firm, melt the milk chocolate in a double boiler. Spread the melted chocolate over the topping, set aside in a cool place, then cut the shortbread into squares or bars to serve.

Vanilla Hearts

Makes about 16

INGREDIENTS

2 cups all-purpose flour

$^2/_3$ cup butter, cut into small pieces

$^1/_2$ cup superfine sugar

1 tsp vanilla extract

superfine sugar, for dusting

1 Lightly grease a cookie sheet with a little butter.

2 Sift the flour into a large mixing bowl and rub in the butter with your fingers until the mixture is well combined and resembles fine breadcrumbs.

3 Stir in the superfine sugar and vanilla extract and bring the mixture together to make a firm dough.

4 On a lightly floured kitchen surface, roll out the dough to a thickness of about 1 inch. Stamp out 12 heart shapes with a heart-shaped cookie cutter measuring about 2 inches across and 1 inch deep.

5 Arrange the hearts on the prepared cookie sheet. Bake in a preheated oven at 350°F for about 15–20 minutes, until the hearts are a light golden color.

6 Transfer the hearts to a wire rack. Let the cookies cool slightly before serving. Dust the vanilla hearts with a little superfine sugar, if desired.

COOK'S TIP

Place a fresh vanilla bean in your superfine sugar and keep it in a storage jar for several weeks to give the sugar a delicious vanilla flavor.

Rock Drops

Makes 8

INGREDIENTS

1¾ cups all-purpose flour
2 tsp baking powder
⅓ cup butter, cut into small pieces

⅓ cup raw crystal sugar
½ cup golden raisins
2 tbsp candied cherries,
    finely chopped

1 egg, beaten
2 tbsp milk

1 Lightly grease a cookie sheet with a little butter or margarine.

2 Sift the flour and baking powder into a large mixing bowl. Rub in the butter with your fingers until well combined and the mixture resembles breadcrumbs.

3 Stir in the raw crystal sugar, golden raisins, and chopped candied cherries, combining all the ingredients thoroughly.

4 Add the beaten egg and the milk to the mixture and mix to form a soft dough.

5 Spoon 8 mounds of the mixture onto the cookie sheet, spacing them well apart as they will spread while they are cooking.

6 Bake in a preheated oven at 400°F for 15–20 minutes, until firm to the touch when pressed with a finger.

7 Remove the rock drops from the cookie sheet. You can either serve them piping hot from the oven or transfer them to a wire rack and let cool before serving.

COOK'S TIP

For convenience, prepare the dry ingredients in advance and just before cooking stir in the liquid.

Chocolate Chip Brownies

Makes 12

INGREDIENTS

5¹/₂ ounces dark chocolate, broken
into pieces
1 cup butter, softened
2 cups self-rising flour

¹/₂ cup superfine sugar
4 eggs, beaten
³/₄ cup chopped pistachio nuts

3¹/₂ ounces white chocolate,
roughly chopped
confectioners' sugar, for dusting

1 Lightly grease a 9-inch baking pan and line with wax paper.

2 Melt the dark chocolate and butter in a double boiler. Leave to cool slightly.

3 Sift the flour into a separate mixing bowl and stir in the superfine sugar.

4 Stir the eggs into the melted chocolate mixture, then pour this mixture into the flour and sugar mixture, beating well. Stir in the pistachio nuts and white chocolate, then pour the mixture into the pan, spreading it evenly into the corners.

5 Bake in a preheated oven at 350°F for 30–35 minutes, until firm to the touch. Cool in the pan for about 20 minutes, then turn out onto a wire rack to cool further.

6 Dust the surface of the cookies with a little confectioners' sugar and cut into 12 pieces when completely cold and crisp.

COOK'S TIP

The brownie won't be completely firm in the middle when it is removed from the oven, but it will set when it has cooled.

Chocolate Biscotti

Makes 16

INGREDIENTS

1 egg
1⅓ cup superfine sugar
1 tsp vanilla extract

1 cup all-purpose flour
½ tsp baking powder
1 tsp ground cinnamon

1¾ ounces dark chocolate,
    roughly chopped
½ cup toasted slivered almonds
½ cup pine nuts

1 Grease a large cookie sheet with butter.

2 Beat the egg, sugar, and vanilla extract in a mixing bowl with an electric mixer until it is thick and pale—ribbons of mixture should trail from the beater as you lift it.

3 Sift the flour, baking powder, and cinnamon into a separate bowl, then sift into the egg mixture and fold in gently. Stir in the chocolate, slivered almonds, and pine nuts.

4 Turn out onto a lightly floured surface and shape into a flat log about 9 inches long and ¾ inch wide. Transfer to the prepared cookie sheet.

5 Bake in a preheated oven at 350°F for 20–25 minutes, or until golden. Remove from the oven and cool for 5 minutes, or until firm.

6 Transfer the log to a cutting board. Using a serrated bread knife, cut the log on the diagonal into slices about ½ inch thick and arrange them on the cookie sheet. Cook for 10–15 minutes, turning halfway through the cooking time.

7 Cool for about 5 minutes, then transfer to a wire rack to cool completely.

Chocolate Macaroons

Makes 18

INGREDIENTS

2 3/4 ounces dark chocolate, broken
into pieces

2 egg whites

pinch of salt

1 cup superfine sugar

1 1/4 cups ground almonds

shredded coconut, for sprinkling
(optional)

1 Grease 2 cookie sheets with a little butter or margarine and line with baking parchment or rice paper.

2 Melt the dark chocolate pieces in a double boiler, then cool slightly.

3 In a mixing bowl, beat the egg whites with the salt until they form soft peaks.

4 Gradually whisk the superfine sugar into the egg whites, then fold in the ground almonds and cooled melted chocolate until all the ingredients are thoroughly incorporated.

5 Place heaping teaspoonfuls of the mixture on the prepared cookie sheets, spacing them well apart, and spread into drops about 2 1/2 inches across. Sprinkle with a little shredded coconut, if desired.

6 Bake in a preheated oven at 300°F for about 25 minutes, or until the macaroons are firm to the touch when pressed with a finger.

7 Cool slightly before carefully lifting the chocolate macaroons from the cookie sheets. Transfer to a wire rack and cool completely before serving.

COOK'S TIP

Store the macaroons in an airtight container and eat within 1 week.

Florentines

Makes 8–10

INGREDIENTS

4 tbsp butter
$^1/_4$ cup superfine sugar
$2^1/_4$ cup all-purpose flour, sifted

$^1/_3$ cup almonds, chopped
$^1/_3$ cup chopped candied peel
$^1/_4$ cup raisins, chopped

2 tbsp candied cherries, chopped
finely grated rind of $^1/_2$ lemon
$4^1/_2$ ounces dark chocolate, melted

1 Line 2 large cookie sheets with baking parchment.

2 Heat the butter and superfine sugar in a small saucepan until the butter has just melted and the sugar dissolved. Remove the pan from the heat.

3 Stir in the flour and mix until well combined. Stir in the chopped almonds, candied peel, raisins, cherries and lemon rind and mix together well.

Place teaspoonfuls of the mixture well apart on the cookie sheets.

4 Bake in a preheated oven at 350°F for 10 minutes, or until lightly golden in color.

5 As soon as the florentines are removed from the oven, press the edges into neat shapes while still on the cookie sheets, using a cookie cutter. Cool on the cookie sheets until firm, then

carefully transfer to a wire rack to cool completely.

6 Spread the melted chocolate over the smooth side of each florentine. As the chocolate begins to set, mark wavy lines or the pattern of your choice in it with a fork. Leave the florentines until set, chocolate side up.

Meringues

Makes about 13

INGREDIENTS

4 egg whites	¹/₂ cup sugar	1¹/₄ cups heavy cream,
pinch of salt	¹/₂ cup superfine sugar	whipped lightly

1 Line 3 cookie sheets with a few sheets of baking parchment.

2 In a large clean bowl, whisk together the egg whites and salt until they are stiff, using an electric mixer. (You should be able to turn the bowl upside down without any movement from the egg whites.)

3 Carefully beat the sugar into the egg white mixture a little at a time; the meringue should start to look glossy at this stage.

4 Sprinkle in the superfine sugar, a little at a time, and continue beating until all the sugar has been incorporated and the meringue is thick, white, and stands in tall peaks.

5 Transfer the meringue mixture to a pastry bag fitted with a ³/₄-inch star tip. Pipe about 26 small whirls onto the prepared cookie sheets.

6 Bake in a preheated oven at 250°F for about 1¹/₂ hours, or until the meringues are pale golden in color and can be easily lifted off the paper. Let the meringues cool in the turned-off oven overnight.

7 Just before serving, sandwich the meringues together in pairs with the whipped heavy cream and arrange on a serving plate.

VARIATION

For a finer texture, replace the ordinary sugar with superfine sugar.

Puddings & Desserts

No true meal is really complete without a pudding, and this chapter indulges the reader with a hearty and wholesome collection of some of the best-loved family favorites. Fruit puddings, chocolate puddings, lemon puddings, and crumbly puddings—they are all fun, easy to make, and deliciously delightful to eat. This chapter also offers some new surprises for old-fashioned puddings, leaving you with the difficult decision of which to try first.

Chocolate is comforting at anytime, but no more so than when served in a steaming hot pudding. It is hard to think of anything more warming, comforting, and homely than tucking into a steamed hot chocolate pudding on a cold day. The child in us will love the chocolate addition to nursery favorites such as Bread & Butter Pudding. In fact, there are several old favorites that have been given the chocolate treatment, bringing them bang up-to-date, and putting them on the chocolate lover's map.

Chocolate Queen of Puddings

Serves 4

INGREDIENTS

1³/₄ ounces dark chocolate

2 cups chocolate-flavored milk

1³/₄ cups fresh white or whole-wheat breadcrumbs

¹/₂ cup superfine sugar

2 eggs, separated

4 tbsp black cherry preserve

1 Break the chocolate into small pieces and place in a saucepan with the chocolate-flavored milk. Heat gently, stirring until the chocolate melts. Bring almost to a boil, then remove the pan from the heat.

2 Place the breadcrumbs in a large mixing bowl with 5 tsp of the superfine sugar. Pour the chocolate milk over the breadcrumb mixture and mix well. Beat in the egg yolks.

3 Spoon into a 5-cup pie dish and bake in a preheated oven at 350°F for 25–30 minutes, or until set and firm to the touch.

4 Beat the egg whites in a large grease-free bowl until standing in soft peaks. Gradually beat in the remaining superfine sugar and continue beating until you have a glossy, thick meringue.

5 Spread the black cherry preserve over the surface of the chocolate mixture and pile or pipe the meringue on top. Return the pudding to the oven for about 15 minutes, or until the meringue is crisp and golden.

VARIATION

If you wish, add ¹/₂ cup shredded coconut to the breadcrumbs and omit the preserve.

Chocolate Eve's Pudding with Bitter Chocolate Sauce

Serves 4

INGREDIENTS

1¼ cups fresh or frozen raspberries, thawed if frozen

2 eating apples

4 tbsp seedless raspberry preserve

2 tbsp port (optional)

SPONGE TOPPING:

4 tbsp soft margarine

4 tbsp superfine sugar

²⁄₃ cup self-rising flour, sifted

1¾ ounces white chocolate, grated

1 egg

2 tbsp milk

BITTER CHOCOLATE SAUCE:

3 ounces dark chocolate, broken into small pieces

²⁄₃ cup light cream

1 Peel, core, and thickly slice the apples. Place the slices of apple and the raspberries in a shallow 5-cup ovenproof dish.

2 Place the raspberry preserve and port (if using) in a small pan and heat gently until the preserve melts and combines thoroughly with the port. Remove from the heat and pour the mixture over the fruit.

3 Place the margarine, sugar, flour, grated white chocolate, egg, and milk in a large mixing bowl and beat well until the mixture is smooth.

4 Spoon the sponge mixture over the fruit and level the surface. Bake in a preheated oven at 350°F for 40–45 minutes, or until the sponge is golden and springy to the touch.

5 To make the sauce, place the chocolate in a heavy-based saucepan with the cream. Heat gently, beating until smooth. Serve warm with the dessert.

VARIATION

Use dark chocolate in the sponge and top with apricot halves, covered with peach schnapps and apricot conserve.

Mini Chocolate Ginger Puddings with Chocolate Custard

Serves 4

INGREDIENTS

¹/₂ cup soft margarine
³/₄ cup self-rising flour, sifted
7 tbsp superfine sugar
2 eggs
¹/₄ cup unsweetened cocoa, sifted

1 ounce dark chocolate
1³/₄ ounces preserved ginger

CHOCOLATE CUSTARD:
2 egg yolks
1 tbsp superfine sugar
1 tbsp cornstarch

1¹/₄ cups milk
3¹/₂ ounces dark chocolate, broken
    into pieces
confectioners' sugar, to dust

1 Lightly grease 4 individual pudding basins. Place the margarine, flour, sugar, eggs, and cocoa powder in a mixing bowl and beat until well combined and smooth. Chop the chocolate and ginger and stir into the mixture.

2 Spoon the cake mixture into the prepared basins and level the top. The mixture should three-quarters fill the basins. Cover the basins with discs of baking parchment and cover with a pleated sheet of foil. Steam for 45 minutes until the puddings are cooked and springy to the touch.

3 Meanwhile, make the custard. Beat together the egg yolks, sugar, and cornstarch to form a smooth paste. Heat the milk until boiling and pour over the egg mixture. Return to the pan and cook over a very low heat stirring until thick. Remove from the heat and beat in the chocolate. Stir until the chocolate melts.

4 Lift the puddings from the steamer, run a knife around the edge of the basins, and turn out onto serving plates. Dust with sugar and drizzle some chocolate custard over the top.

Chocolate Bread & Butter Pudding

Serves 4

INGREDIENTS

8 ounces brioche	1 egg	4 tbsp superfine sugar
1 tbsp butter	2 egg yolks	15 ounce can light evaporated milk
1¾ ounces dark chocolate chips		

1 Cut the brioche into thin slices. Lightly butter one side of each slice.

2 Place a layer of brioche, buttered side down, in the bottom of a shallow ovenproof dish. Sprinkle a few chocolate chips over the top.

3 Continue layering the brioche and chocolate chips, finishing with a layer of bread on top.

4 Beat together the egg, egg yolks, and sugar until well combined. Heat the milk in a small saucepan until it just begins to simmer.

Gradually add it to the egg mixture, beating well.

5 Pour the custard over the pudding and let stand for 5 minutes. Press the brioche down into the milk.

6 Place in a roasting pan and fill with boiling water to come halfway up the side of the dish (this is known as a bain-marie).

7 Bake in a preheated oven at 350°F for 30 minutes, or until the custard has set. Let cool for 5 minutes before serving. Alternatively, serve cold.

VARIATION

For a double-chocolate pudding, heat the milk with 1 tbsp of unsweetened cocoa, stirring until well dissolved, then continue from step 4.

COOK'S TIP

The pudding can be prepared a few hours ahead and baked when required.

Chocolate French Toasties

Serves 4–6

INGREDIENTS

1³/₄ ounces dark chocolate
²/₃ cup milk
1 egg
4 tbsp seedless raspberry preserve

2 tbsp rum (optional)
8 thick slices white bread
butter or oil, for frying
¹/₂ tsp ground cinnamon

3 tbsp superfine sugar
a little whipped cream, to serve

1 Break the chocolate into small pieces and place in a small pan with the milk. Heat gently, stirring until the chocolate melts. Let cool slightly.

2 Beat the egg in a large mixing bowl and beat in the warm chocolate milk.

3 Heat the raspberry preserve gently and stir in the rum, if using. Set aside and keep warm.

4 Remove the crusts from the bread, cut into triangles, and dip each one into the chocolate mixture.

Heat the butter or oil in a skillet and fry the bread triangles for 2–3 minutes, until just crispy, turning once.

5 Mix together the cinnamon and superfine sugar and sprinkle it over the toast. Serve with the hot preserve sauce and a little whipped cream.

VARIATION

If you wish, try this recipe using brioche or fruit bread for a tasty variation.

COOK'S TIP

Young children adore this dessert. Cut the bread into fingers to make it easier for them to handle.

Chocolate Fudge Pudding

Serves 6

INGREDIENTS

³/₄ cup soft margarine
1 ¹/₄ cups self-rising flour
¹/₂ cup light corn syrup
3 eggs
¹/₄ cup unsweetened cocoa

CHOCOLATE FUDGE SAUCE:
3 ¹/₂ ounces dark chocolate
¹/₂ cup sweetened condensed milk
4 tbsp heavy cream

1 Lightly grease a 5-cup heatproof bowl.

2 Place the ingredients for the sponge in a mixing bowl and beat until well combined and smooth.

3 Spoon into the prepared bowl and level the top. Cover with baking parchment and tie a pleated sheet of foil over the bowl. Steam for 1¹/₂–2 hours, until the pudding is cooked and springy to the touch.

4 To make the sauce, break the chocolate into small pieces, and place in a small pan with the condensed milk. Heat gently, stirring until the chocolate melts.

5 Remove the pan from the heat and stir in the heavy cream, mixing well.

6 To serve the pudding, turn it out onto a serving plate and pour over a little of the chocolate fudge sauce. Serve the remaining sauce separately.

COOK'S TIP

To cook the dessert in the microwave, cook it, uncovered, on high for 4 minutes, turning the bowl once. Let stand for at least 5 minutes before turning out. While the pudding is standing, make the sauce. Break the chocolate into pieces and place in a microwave-safe bowl with the milk. Cook on high for 1 minute, then stir until the chocolate melts. Stir in the heavy cream and serve.

Chocolate Fruit Crumble

Serves 4

INGREDIENTS

14 ounce can apricots, in
  natural juice
1 pound cooking apples, peeled and
  thickly sliced

³/4 cup all-purpose flour
¹/3 cup butter
²/3 cup dried oats
4 tbsp superfine sugar

²/3 cup chocolate chips

1 Lightly grease
an ovenproof dish with
a little butter or margarine.

2 Drain the apricots,
reserving 4 tbsp of
the juice. Place the apples
and apricots in the prepared
ovenproof dish with
the reserved apricot juice
and toss to mix.

3 Sift the flour into a
mixing bowl. Cut the
butter into small cubes and
rub it in with your fingertips
until the mixture resembles
fine breadcrumbs. Stir in
the dried oats, sugar, and
chocolate chips.

4 Sprinkle the crumble
mixture over the apples
and apricots and level the
top roughly. Do not press
the crumble into the fruit.

5 Bake in a preheated
oven at 350°F for
40–45 minutes, or until
the topping is golden.
Serve hot or cold.

COOK'S TIP

*You can use dark,
milk, or white chocolate
chips in this recipe or a
mixture of all three.*

VARIATION

*For a double chocolate
crumble, replace 1–2
tablespoons of flour with
unsweetened cocoa.*

VARIATION

*Other fruits can be used to
make this crumble — fresh
pears mixed with fresh or
frozen raspberries work well.
If you do not use canned fruit,
add 4 tablespoons of orange
juice to the fresh fruit.*

246

Poached Pears with Mascarpone Chocolate Sauce

Serves 6

INGREDIENTS

à6 firm ripe pears	rind of 1 orange	CHOCOLATE SAUCE:
7 tbsp superfine sugar	2 cloves	6 ounces dark chocolate
2 cinnamon sticks	1 bottle rosé wine	1¼ cups mascarpone cheese
		2 tbsp orange-flavored liqueur

1 Carefully peel the pears, leaving the stalk intact.

2 Place the sugar, cinnamon sticks, orange rind, cloves, and wine in a saucepan that will hold the 6 pears snugly.

3 Heat gently until the sugar has dissolved, then add the pears to the liquid, and bring to a simmer. Cover and poach gently for 20 minutes. If serving them cold, leave the pears to cool in the liquid, then chill until required.

If serving hot, leave the pears in the hot liquid while preparing the chocolate sauce.

4 To make the sauce, melt the chocolate. Beat together the cheese and the orange-flavored liqueur. Beat the cheese mixture into the chocolate.

5 Remove the pears from the poaching liquid and place on a serving plate. Add a generous spoonful of sauce on the side and serve the remainder separately.

COOK'S TIP

There is no need to waste the tasty poaching liquid. Boil it rapidly in a clean pan for about 10 minutes to reduce to a syrup. Use the syrup to sweeten a fresh fruit salad or spoon it over ice cream.

COOK'S TIP

Rosettes of cream can be piped onto the dessert, if desired.

Saucy Chocolate Pudding

Serves 4

INGREDIENTS

1¼ cups milk
2¾ ounces dark chocolate
½ tsp vanilla extract
1 cup 1 tbsp superfine sugar

½ cup butter
1¼ cups self-rising flour
2 tbsp unsweetened cocoa
confectioners' sugar, to dust

FOR THE SAUCE:
3 tbsp unsweetened cocoa
4 tbsp light brown sugar
1¼ cups boiling water

1 Lightly grease a 3¾-cup ovenproof dish.

2 Place the milk in a small pan. Break the chocolate into pieces and add to the milk. Heat gently, stirring until the chocolate melts. Let cool slightly. Stir in the vanilla extract.

3 Beat together the superfine sugar and butter in a bowl until light and fluffy. Sift the flour and unsweetened cocoa together. Add to the bowl with the chocolate milk and beat until smooth, using an electric beater if you have one. Pour the mixture into the prepared dish.

4 To make the sauce, mix together the unsweetened cocoa and sugar. Add a little boiling water and mix to a smooth paste, then stir in the remaining water. Pour the sauce over the pudding, but do not mix in.

5 Place the dish on a cookie sheet and bake in a preheated oven at 350°F for 40 minutes, or until dry on top and springy to the touch. Let stand for about 5 minutes, then dust with a little confectioners' sugar just before serving.

VARIATION

For a mocha sauce, add 1 tbsp instant coffee to the cocoa and sugar in step 4, before mixing to a paste with boiling water.

Pecan & Chocolate Fudge Ring

Serves 6

INGREDIENTS

FUDGE SAUCE:
3 tbsp butter
3 tbsp light brown sugar
4 tbsp light corn syrup

2 tbsp milk
1 tbsp unsweetened cocoa
1¹/2 ounces dark chocolate
¹/2 cup finely chopped pecans

CAKE:
¹/2 cup soft margarine
7 tbsp light brown sugar
1 cup self-rising flour
2 eggs
2 tbsp milk
1 tbsp light corn syrup

1 Lightly grease an 8-inch ring pan.

2 To make the fudge sauce, place the butter, sugar, syrup, milk, and unsweetened cocoa in a small pan and heat gently, stirring until combined.

3 Break the chocolate into pieces, add to the mixture, and stir until melted. Stir in the chopped nuts. Pour into the base of the pan and set aside to cool.

4 To make the cake, place all the ingredients in a mixing bowl and beat until smooth. Carefully spoon the cake mixture over the chocolate fudge sauce.

5 Bake in a preheated oven at 350°F for 35 minutes, or until the cake is cooked through and springy to the touch.

6 Cool in the pan for 5 minutes, then turn out on to a serving dish and serve.

COOK'S TIP

To make in the microwave, place the butter, sugar, syrup, milk, and unsweetened cocoa for the sauce in a microwave-safe bowl. Cook on high for 2 minutes, stirring twice. Stir in the chocolate until melted, then add the nuts. Pour into a 5-cup microwave-safe ring mold. Make the cake and cook on high for 3–4 minutes, until just dry on top; let stand for 5 minutes.

Chocolate Meringue Pie

Serves 6

INGREDIENTS

8 ounces dark chocolate graham crackers 4 tbsp butter	FILLING: 3 egg yolks 4 tbsp superfine sugar 4 tbsp cornstarch 2¹/₂ cups milk 3¹/₂ ounces dark chocolate, melted	MERINGUE: 2 egg whites 7 tbsp superfine sugar ¹/₄ tsp vanilla extract

1 Place the graham crackers in a plastic bag and crush with a rolling pin. Pour into a mixing bowl. Melt the butter and stir it into the cracker crumbs until well mixed. Press the cookie mixture firmly into the base and up the sides of a 9-inch flan pan or dish.

2 To make the filling, beat the egg yolks, superfine sugar, and cornstarch in a large bowl until they form a smooth paste, adding a little of the milk if necessary.

Heat the milk until almost boiling, then slowly pour it into the egg mixture, constantly beating well.

3 Return the mixture to the saucepan and cook gently, beating constantly, until it thickens. Remove from the heat. Beat in the melted chocolate, then pour it onto the graham cracker base.

4 To make the meringue, beat the egg whites in a large mixing bowl until standing in soft peaks. Gradually beat in about

two-thirds of the sugar until the mixture is stiff and glossy. Fold in the remaining sugar and the vanilla extract.

5 Spread the meringue over the filling, covering it completely and swirling the surface with the back of a spoon to give it an attractive finish. Bake in the center of a preheated oven at 375°F for about 30 minutes, or until the meringue is golden. Serve hot or just warm.

Chocolate Apple Pie

Serves 6

INGREDIENTS

CHOCOLATE PIE CRUST:
4 tbsp unsweetened cocoa
1³/₄ cups all-purpose flour
2 egg yolks
¹/₂ cup softened butter
4 tbsp superfine sugar
few drops of vanilla extract
cold water, to mix

FILLING:
1 pound 10 ounces cooking apples
2 tbsp butter
¹/₂ tsp ground cinnamon
³/₄ cup dark chocolate chips

a little egg white, beaten
¹/₂ tsp superfine sugar
whipped cream or vanilla ice cream,
   to serve

1 To make the crust, sift the unsweetened cocoa and flour into a mixing bowl and rub in the butter until the mixture resembles fine breadcrumbs. Stir in the sugar. Add the egg yolk, vanilla extract, and enough water to mix to a dough.

2 Roll out the dough on a lightly floured surface and use to line a deep 8-inch flan or cake pan. Chill for 30 minutes. Roll out any trimmings and cut out some pastry leaves to decorate the top of the pie.

3 Peel, core, and thickly slice the apples. Place half the slices in a saucepan with the butter and cinnamon and cook over a gentle heat, stirring occasionally, until the apples soften.

4 Stir in the uncooked apple slices, let cool slightly, then stir in the chocolate chips.

Prick the base of the pie shell with a fork and pile the apple mixture into it. Arrange the pastry leaves decoratively on top. Brush the leaves with a little egg white and sprinkle with superfine sugar.

5 Bake in a preheated oven at 350°F for 35 minutes, until the pastry is golden and crisp. Serve warm or cold, with whipped cream or vanilla ice cream.

Chocolate Pear & Almond Flan

Serves 6

INGREDIENTS

³/₄ cup all-purpose flour
¹/₄ cup ground almonds
¹/₄ cup margarine
about 3 tbsp water

FILLING:
14 ounce can pear halves, in
    natural juice
4 tbsp butter
4 tbsp superfine sugar
2 eggs, beaten
1 cup ground almonds
2 tbsp unsweetened cocoa
few drops of almond extract
confectioners' sugar, to dust

CHOCOLATE SAUCE:
4 tbsp superfine sugar
3 tbsp light corn syrup
¹/₃ cup water
6 ounces dark chocolate, broken
    into pieces
2 tbsp butter

1 Lightly grease an 8-inch flan pan. Sift the flour into a mixing bowl and stir in the almonds. Rub in the margarine with your fingertips until the mixture resembles breadcrumbs. Add enough water to mix to a soft dough. Cover, chill in the freezer for 10 minutes, then roll out, and use to line the pan. Prick the base and chill.

2 To make the filling, drain the pears well. Beat the butter and sugar until light and fluffy. Beat in the eggs. Fold in the almonds, unsweetened cocoa, and extract. Spread the chocolate mixture in the pie shell and arrange the pears on top, pressing down lightly. Bake in the center of a preheated oven at 400°F for 30 minutes, or until the filling has risen.

Cool slightly and transfer to a serving dish, if preferred. Dust with sugar.

3 To make the sauce, place the sugar, syrup, and water in a pan and heat gently, stirring until the sugar dissolves. Boil gently for 1 minute. Remove the pan from the heat, add the chocolate and butter, and stir until melted. Serve with the flan.

Chocolate & Banana Crêpes

Serves 4

INGREDIENTS

3 large bananas	HOT CHOCOLATE SAUCE:	CRÊPES:
6 tbsp orange juice	1 tbsp unsweetened cocoa	1 cup all-purpose flour
grated rind of 1 orange	2 tsp cornstarch	1 tbsp unsweetened cocoa
2 tbsp orange- or banana-	3 tbsp milk	1 egg
flavored liqueur	1¹/₂ ounces dark chocolate	1 tsp sunflower oil
	1 tbsp butter	1¹/₄ cups milk
	¹/₂ cup light corn syrup	oil, for frying
	¹/₄ tsp vanilla extract	

1 Peel and slice the bananas and arrange them in a dish with the orange juice and rind and the liqueur. Set aside.

2 Mix the unsweetened cocoa and cornstarch in a bowl, then stir in the milk. Break the dark chocolate into pieces and place in a pan with the butter and light corn syrup. Heat gently, stirring until well blended. Add the cocoa mixture and bring to a boil over a gentle heat, stirring.

Simmer for 1 minute, then remove from the heat and stir in the vanilla extract.

3 To make the crêpes, sift the flour and cocoa into a mixing bowl and make a well in the center. Add the egg and oil. Gradually beat in the milk to form a smooth batter. Heat a little oil in a heavy-based skillet and pour off any excess. Pour in a little batter and tilt the pan to coat the base. Cook over a medium heat until the underside is browned.

Flip over and cook the other side. Slide the crêpe out of the pan and keep warm. Repeat until all the batter has been used.

4 To serve, reheat the chocolate sauce for 1-2 minutes. Fill the crêpes with the bananas and fold in half or into triangles. Pour a little chocolate sauce on top and serve.

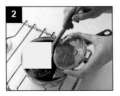

Chocolate Apple Pancake Stack

Serves 4–6

INGREDIENTS

2 cups all-purpose flour
1½ tsp baking powder
4 tbsp superfine sugar
1 egg

1 tbsp butter, melted
1¼ cups milk
1 eating apple
⅓ cup dark chocolate chips

Hot Chocolate Sauce or maple
syrup, to serve

1 Sift the flour and baking powder into a mixing bowl. Stir in the superfine sugar. Make a well in the center and add the egg and melted butter. Gradually beat in the milk and continue beating to form a smooth batter.

2 Peel, core, and grate the apple and stir it into the batter with the chocolate chips.

3 Heat a griddle or heavy-based skillet over a medium heat and grease it lightly. For each pancake, place about 2 tablespoons of the batter onto the griddle or skillet and spread to make a 3-inch round.

4 Cook for a few minutes, until you see bubbles appear on the surface of the pancake. Turn over and cook for a further 1 minute. Remove from the pan and keep warm. Repeat with the remaining batter to make about 12 pancakes.

5 To serve, stack 2 or 3 pancakes on an individual serving plate and serve with chocolate sauce or maple syrup.

COOK'S TIP

To keep the cooked pancakes warm, pile them on top of each other with baking parchment in between to prevent them from sticking to each other.

VARIATION

Milk chocolate chips can be used instead of the dark ones, if preferred.

Chocolate Fondue

Serves 6–8

INGREDIENTS

CHOCOLATE FONDUE:
8 ounces dark chocolate
³/₄ cup heavy cream
2 tbsp brandy

TO SERVE:
selection of fruit
white and pink marshmallows
sweet cookies

1 Break the chocolate into small pieces and place in a small saucepan, together with the heavy cream.

2 Heat the mixture gently, stirring constantly, until the chocolate has melted and blended with the cream.

3 Remove the pan from the heat and stir in the brandy.

4 Pour into a fondue pot or a small flameproof dish and keep warm, preferably over a small burner.

5 Serve with a selection of fruit, marshmallows, and cookies for dipping. The fruit and marshmallows can be spiked on fondue forks, wooden skewers, or ordinary forks for dipping into the chocolate fondue.

COOK'S TIP

To prepare the fruit for dipping, cut larger fruit into bite-size pieces. Fruit that discolors, such as bananas, apples, and pears, should be dipped in a little lemon juice as soon as it is cut.

COOK'S TIP

It is not essential to use a special fondue set. Dish warmers that use a night light are just as good for keeping the fondue warm. If you do not have one, stand the fondue dish in a larger dish and pour in enough boiling water to come halfway up the fondue dish. Whichever method you use to keep your fondue warm, place it on a heatproof stand to protect the table.

Hot Chocolate Soufflé

Serves 4

INGREDIENTS

3¹/₂ ounces dark chocolate
1¹/₄ cups milk
2 tbsp butter
4 large eggs, separated
1 tbsp cornstarch

4 tbsp superfine sugar
¹/₂ tsp vanilla extract
²/₃ cup dark chocolate chips
superfine and confectioners' sugar,
to dust

CHOCOLATE CUSTARD:
2 tbsp cornstarch
1 tbsp superfine sugar
2 cups milk
1³/₄ ounces dark chocolate

1 Grease a 5-cup soufflé dish and sprinkle with superfine sugar. Break the chocolate into small pieces.

2 Heat the milk with the butter in a pan until almost boiling. Mix the egg yolks, cornstarch, and superfine sugar in a bowl and pour in some of the hot milk, beating. Return the mixture to the pan and cook gently, stirring constantly, until thickened. Add the chocolate and stir until melted. Remove the pan from the heat and stir in the extract.

3 Beat the egg whites until standing in soft peaks. Fold half the egg whites into the chocolate mixture. Fold in the rest with the chocolate chips. Pour into the dish and bake in a preheated oven at 350°F for 40–45 minutes, until well risen.

4 Meanwhile, make the custard. Put the cornstarch and sugar in a small bowl and mix to a smooth paste with a little of the milk. Heat the remaining milk until almost boiling. Pour a little of the hot milk

into the cornstarch, mix well, then pour it back into the pan. Cook gently, stirring, until thickened. Break the chocolate into pieces and add to the custard, stirring until melted.

5 Dust the soufflé with sugar and serve immediately with the chocolate custard.

Chocolate Zabaglione

Serves 2

INGREDIENTS

4 egg yolks
4 tbsp superfine sugar
1³/₄ ounces dark chocolate

1 cup Marsala
unsweetened cocoa, to dust

1 Using an electric handmixer beat together the egg yolks and superfine sugar in a large glass mixing bowl until you have a very pale mixture.

2 Grate the chocolate finely and fold it into the egg mixture. Fold in the Marsala.

3 Place the mixing bowl over a saucepan of gently simmering water and set the mixer on the lowest speed. Cook gently, beating continuously, until the mixture thickens; take care not to overcook or the mixture will curdle.

4 Spoon the hot mixture into warm individual glass dishes and dust lightly with unsweetened cocoa. Serve the zabaglione as soon as possible while it is warm, light, and fluffy.

COOK'S TIP

Spoon the zabaglione into coffee cups and serve with amaretti cookies to the side of the saucer.

COOK'S TIP

Make the dessert just before serving, as the mixture will separate if left to stand. If it begins to curdle, you may be able to save it if you remove it from the heat immediately and place it in a bowl of cold water to stop the cooking. Beat vigorously until the mixture comes together.

Chocolate Mint Swirl

Serves 6

1¼ cups heavy cream
²/₃ cup creamy fromage frais or
   thick unsweetened yogurt

2 tbsp confectioners' sugar
1 tbsp crème de menthe
6 ounces dark chocolate

chocolate, to decorate

1 Place the cream in a large mixing bowl and beat until standing in soft peaks.

2 Fold in the fromage frais or yogurt and sugar, then place about one-third of the mixture in a smaller bowl. Stir the crème de menthe into the smaller bowl. Melt the dark chocolate and stir it into the remaining mixture.

3 Place alternate spoon-fuls of the 2 mixtures into serving glasses, then swirl the mixture together to give a decorative effect. Chill until required.

4 To make the piped chocolate decorations, melt a small amount of chocolate and place in a paper pastry bag.

5 Place a sheet of baking parchment on a board and pipe squiggles, stars, or flower shapes with the melted chocolate. Alternatively, to make curved decorations, pipe decorations onto a long strip of baking parchment, then carefully place the strip over a rolling pin, securing with tape. Allow the chocolate to set, then carefully remove from the baking parchment.

6 Decorate each dessert with piped chocolate decorations and serve. The desserts can be decorated and then chilled, if desired.

COOK'S TIP

Pipe the patterns freehand or draw patterns onto baking parchment first, turn the parchment over, and then pipe the chocolate, following the drawn outline.

Chocolate Rum Pots

Serves 6

INGREDIENTS

8 ounces dark chocolate

4 eggs, separated

$^1/_3$ cup superfine sugar

4 tbsp dark rum

4 tbsp heavy cream

TO DECORATE:

a little whipped cream

chocolate shapes

1 Melt the chocolate and let cool slightly.

2 Beat the egg yolks with the superfine sugar in a bowl until very pale and fluffy; this will take about 5 minutes with an electric mixer.

3 Drizzle the chocolate into the mixture and fold it in, together with the rum and the heavy cream.

4 Beat the egg whites in a grease-free bowl until standing in soft peaks. Fold the egg whites into the chocolate mixture in 2 batches. Divide the mixture between 6 custard pots or other individual dishes, and chill for at least 2 hours.

5 To serve, decorate with a little whipped cream and small chocolate shapes.

COOK'S TIP

Make sure you use a perfectly clean and grease-free bowl for beating the egg whites. They will not aerate if any grease is present, as the smallest amount breaks down the bubbles in the whites, preventing them from trapping and holding air.

VARIATION

These delicious little pots can be flavored with brandy instead of rum, if desired.

Chocolate & Vanilla Creams

Serves 4

INGREDIENTS

2 cups heavy cream	2 tsp gelatin	MARBLED CHOCOLATE SHAPES:
$\frac{1}{3}$ cup superfine sugar	3 tbsp water	a little melted white chocolate
1 vanilla bean	$1\frac{3}{4}$ ounces dark chocolate	a little melted dark chocolate
$\frac{3}{4}$ cup crème fraîche or sour cream		

1 Place the cream and sugar in a saucepan. Cut the vanilla bean into 2 pieces and add to the cream. Heat gently, stirring, until the sugar has dissolved, then bring to a boil. Reduce the heat and simmer for 2–3 minutes.

2 Remove the pan from the heat and take out the vanilla bean. Stir in the crème fraîche or sour cream.

3 Sprinkle the gelatin over the water in a small heatproof bowl and allow to become spongy, then place over a pan of hot water and stir until dissolved. Stir into the cream mixture. Pour half of this mixture into another mixing bowl.

4 Melt the dark chocolate and stir it into one half of the cream mixture. Pour the chocolate mixture into 4 glass serving dishes and chill for 15–20 minutes, until just set. Keep the vanilla mixture at room temperature.

5 Spoon the vanilla mixture on top of the chocolate mixture and chill until the vanilla is set.

6 Meanwhile, make the shapes for the decoration. Spoon the melted white chocolate into a paper pastry bag and snip off the tip. Spread some melted dark chocolate on a piece of baking parchment. While still wet, pipe a fine line of white chocolate in a scribble over the top. Use the tip of a toothpick to marble the white chocolate into the dark. When firm but not too hard, cut into shapes with a small shaped cutter or a sharp knife. Chill the shapes until firm, then use to decorate the desserts before serving.

Chocolate Hazelnut Pots

Serves 6

INGREDIENTS

2 eggs	2¹⁄₂ cups milk	TO DECORATE:
2 egg yolks	3 ounces dark chocolate	grated chocolate or large
1 tbsp superfine sugar	4 tbsp chocolate and hazelnut	chocolate curls
1 tsp cornstarch	spread	

1 Beat together the eggs, egg yolks, superfine sugar, and cornstarch until thoroughly combined. Heat the milk until almost boiling.

2 Gradually pour the milk into the eggs, beating as you do so. Melt the chocolate and hazelnut spread in a double boiler, then beat the melted chocolate mixture into the eggs.

3 Pour into 6 small ovenproof dishes and cover the dishes with foil.

Place them in a roasting pan. Fill the pan with boiling water to come halfway up the sides of the dishes.

4 Bake in a preheated oven at 325°F for 35–40 minutes, until the custard is just set. Remove from the pan and cool, then chill until required. Serve decorated with grated chocolate or chocolate curls.

COOK'S TIP

This dish is traditionally made in little pots called pots de crème, which are individual ovenproof dishes with a lid. Custard pots are fine. The dessert can also be made in one large dish; cook for about 1 hour or until set.

COOK'S TIP

The foil lid prevents a skin from forming on the surface of the custards.

Mocha Creams

Serves 4

INGREDIENTS

8 ounces dark chocolate
1 tbsp instant coffee
1¼ cups boiling water
1 envelope gelatin

3 tbsp cold water
1 tsp vanilla extract
1 tbsp coffee-flavored
   liqueur (optional)

1¼ cups heavy cream
4 chocolate coffee beans
8 amaretti cookies

1 Break the chocolate into small pieces and place in a saucepan with the coffee. Stir in the boiling water and heat gently, stirring, until the chocolate melts.

2 Sprinkle the gelatin over the cold water and allow it to become spongy, then beat it into the hot chocolate mixture to dissolve it.

3 Stir in the vanilla extract and coffee-flavored liqueur, if using.

Let cool until it begins to thicken; beat from time to time.

4 Beat the cream until it forms soft peaks, then reserve a little for decorating the desserts, and fold the remainder into the chocolate mixture. Spoon into serving dishes and allow to set.

5 Decorate with the reserved cream and coffee beans and serve with the cookies.

COOK'S TIP

If desired, the dessert can be made in one large serving dish.

VARIATION

To add a delicious almond flavor to the dessert, replace the coffee-flavored liqueur with almond-flavored liqueur.

Layered Chocolate Mousse

Serves 8

INGREDIENTS

3 eggs

1 tsp cornstarch

4 tbsp superfine sugar

1¼ cups milk

1 envelope gelatin

3 tbsp water

1¼ cups heavy cream

2¾ ounces dark chocolate

2¾ ounces white chocolate

2¾ ounces milk chocolate

chocolate caraque, to decorate

1 Line a 1-pound loaf pan with baking parchment. Separate the eggs, putting each egg white in a separate bowl. Place the egg yolks and sugar in a large mixing bowl and beat until well combined. Place the milk in a pan and heat gently, stirring, until almost boiling. Pour the milk into the egg yolks, beating.

2 Set the bowl over a pan of gently simmering water and cook, stirring, until the mixture thickens enough to thinly coat the back of a wooden spoon.

3 Sprinkle the gelatin over the water in a small heatproof bowl and allow to become spongy. Place over a pan of hot water and stir until dissolved. Stir into the hot mixture. Set aside to cool.

4 Whip the cream until just holding its shape. Fold into the egg custard, then divide the mixture into 3. Melt the 3 types of chocolate separately. Fold the dark chocolate into one egg custard portion. Beat one egg white until standing in soft peaks and fold into the dark chocolate custard

until combined. Pour into the prepared pan and level the top. Chill in the coldest part of the refrigerator until just set. Leave the remaining mixtures at room temperature.

5 Fold the white chocolate into another portion of the egg custard. Beat another egg white and fold in. Pour on top of the dark chocolate layer and chill. Repeat with the remaining milk chocolate and egg white. Chill until set. To serve, turn out onto a dish and decorate with chocolate caraque.

Chocolate Marquise

Serves 6

INGREDIENTS

7 ounces dark chocolate
$\frac{1}{2}$ cup butter
3 egg yolks
$\frac{1}{3}$ cup superfine sugar

1 tsp chocolate extract or 1 tbsp
    chocolate-flavored liqueur
1$\frac{1}{4}$ cups heavy cream

TO SERVE:
crème fraîche
chocolate-dipped fruits
unsweetened cocoa, to dust

1 Break the chocolate into pieces. Place the chocolate and butter in a double boiler and stir until melted and well combined. Remove from the heat and set aside to cool.

2 Place the egg yolks in a mixing bowl with the sugar and beat until the mixture becomes pale and fluffy. Using an electric beater on low speed, slowly beat in the cool chocolate mixture. Stir in the chocolate extract or chocolate-flavored liqueur.

3 Whip the cream until just holding its shape. Fold into the chocolate mixture. Spoon into 6 small custard pots or individual metal molds. Chill for at least 2 hours.

4 To serve, turn out the desserts onto individual serving dishes. If you have difficulty turning them out, dip the molds into a bowl of warm water for a few seconds to help the marquise to slip out. Serve with chocolate-dipped fruit and crème fraîche, and dust with unsweetened cocoa.

COOK'S TIP

The slight tartness of the crème fraîche contrasts well with this very rich dessert. Dip the fruit in white chocolate to give a good color contrast.

Iced White Chocolate Terrine

Serves 8–10

INGREDIENTS

2 tbsp sugar
5 tbsp water

10¹/₂ ounces white chocolate
3 eggs, separated

1¹/₄ cups heavy cream

1 Line a 1-pound loaf pan with aluminum foil or plastic wrap, pressing out as many creases as you can.

2 Place the sugar and water in a heavy-based pan and heat gently, stirring constantly, until the sugar has dissolved. Bring to a boil and boil for 1–2 minutes, until syrupy, then remove the pan from the heat.

3 Break the white chocolate into small pieces and stir it into the syrup, continuing to stir until the chocolate has melted and combined with the syrup. Set aside to cool slightly.

4 Beat the egg yolks into the chocolate mixture. Set aside to cool completely.

5 Lightly whip the cream until just holding its shape and fold it into the chocolate mixture.

6 Beat the egg whites in a grease-free bowl until they are standing in soft peaks. Fold into the chocolate mixture. Pour into the prepared loaf pan and freeze for 8 hours or overnight.

7 To serve, remove from the freezer about 10–15 minutes before serving. Turn out of the pan and cut into slices to serve.

COOK'S TIP

To make a coulis, place 8 ounces soft fruit of your choice – strawberries, black or red currants, mango, or raspberries are ideal – in a food processor or blender. Add 1–2 tbsp confectioners' sugar and blend to form a purée. If the fruit contains seeds, rub the purée through a strainer to remove them. Chill until required.

Chocolate Banana Sundae

Serves 4

INGREDIENTS

GLOSSY CHOCOLATE SAUCE:

2 ounces dark chocolate

4 tbsp light corn syrup

1 tbsp butter

1 tbsp brandy or rum (optional)

SUNDAE:

4 bananas

$^2/_3$ cup heavy cream

8–12 scoops of good quality vanilla
ice cream

$^3/_4$ cup slivered or chopped
almonds, toasted

grated or flaked chocolate,
to sprinkle

4 fan wafer cookies

1 To make the chocolate sauce, break the chocolate into small pieces and place in a double boiler with the syrup and butter. Heat until melted, stirring until well combined. Remove the bowl from the heat and stir in the brandy or rum, if using.

2 Slice the bananas and whip the cream until just holding its shape. Place a scoop of ice cream in the bottom of 4 tall sundae dishes. Top with slices of banana, some chocolate sauce, a spoonful of cream, and a generous sprinkling of nuts.

3 Repeat the layers, finishing with a spoonful of cream, sprinkled with nuts and a little grated or flaked chocolate. Serve with fan wafer cookies.

VARIATION

Use half vanilla ice cream and half chocolate ice cream, if desired.

VARIATION

For a traditional banana split, halve the bananas lengthwise and place on a plate with two scoops of ice cream between. Top with cream and sprinkle with nuts. Serve with the glossy chocolate sauce poured over the top.

Rich Chocolate Ice Cream

Serves 6-8

INGREDIENTS

ICE CREAM:
1 egg
3 egg yolks
6 tbsp superfine sugar

1¼ cups milk
9 ounces dark chocolate
1¼ cups heavy cream

TRELLIS CUPS:
3½ ounces dark chocolate

1 Beat together the egg, egg yolks, and superfine sugar in a mixing bowl until thoroughly combined. Heat the milk until almost boiling.

2 Gradually pour the hot milk into the eggs, beating as you do so. Place the bowl over a pan of gently simmering water and cook, stirring, until the mixture thickens sufficiently to thinly coat the back of a wooden spoon.

3 Break the dark chocolate into small pieces and add to the hot

mixture. Stir until the chocolate has melted. Cover with a sheet of dampened baking parchment and let cool.

4 Whip the cream until just holding its shape, then fold into the cooled chocolate mixture. Transfer to a freezer container and freeze for 1-2 hours, until the mixture is frozen 1 inch from the sides.

5 Scrape the ice cream into a chilled bowl and beat again until smooth. Re-freeze until firm.

6 To make the trellis cups, invert a muffin pan and cover 6 alternate mounds with plastic wrap. Melt the chocolate, place it in a paper pastry bag, and snip off the end.

7 Pipe a circle around the base of the mound, then pipe chocolate back and forth over it to form a trellis; carefully pipe a double thickness. Pipe around the base again. Chill until set, then lift from the pan, and remove the plastic wrap. Serve the ice cream in the trellis cups.

Baked Chocolate Alaska

Serves 6

2 eggs	3 egg whites
4 tbsp superfine sugar	2/3 cup superfine sugar
6 tbsp all-purpose flour	4 1/2 cups good quality chocolate
2 tbsp unsweetened cocoa	ice cream

1 Grease a 7-inch round cake pan and line the base with baking parchment.

2 Beat the egg and the superfine sugar in a mixing bowl until very thick and pale. Sift the flour and unsweetened cocoa together and carefully fold into the egg mixture.

3 Pour into the prepared pan and bake in a preheated oven at 425°F for 7 minutes, or until springy to the touch. Transfer to a wire rack to cool completely.

4 Beat the egg whites in a grease-free bowl until they are standing in soft peaks. Gradually add the sugar, beating until you have a thick, glossy meringue.

5 Place the sponge cake on a cookie sheet and pile the ice cream onto the center heaping it up into a dome.

6 Pipe or spread the meringue over the ice cream, making sure the ice cream is completely enclosed. (At this point the dessert can be frozen, if desired.)

7 Return it to the oven, for 5 minutes, until the meringue is just golden. Serve immediately.

COOK'S TIP

This dessert is delicious served with a black currant coulis. Cook a few black currants in a little orange juice until soft, purée, and rub through a strainer. Sweeten to taste with a little confectioners' sugar.

White Chocolate Ice Cream in a Cookie Cup

Serves 6

INGREDIENTS

ICE CREAM:

1 egg

1 egg yolk

3 tbsp superfine sugar

5$\frac{1}{2}$ ounces white chocolate

1$\frac{1}{4}$ cups milk

$\frac{2}{3}$ cup heavy cream

COOKIE CUPS:

1 egg white

4 tbsp superfine sugar

2 tbsp all-purpose flour, sifted

2 tbsp unsweetened cocoa, sifted

2 tbsp butter, melted

1 Place baking parchment on 2 cookie sheets. To make the ice cream, beat the egg, egg yolks, and sugar. Break the chocolate into pieces and melt in a double boiler with 3 tbsp of the milk. Heat the milk until almost boiling and pour into the eggs, beating. Place over a pan of simmering water and cook, stirring, until the mixture thickens enough to coat the back of a wooden spoon.

Beat in the chocolate. Cover with dampened baking parchment and cool.

2 Whip the cream until just holding its shape and fold into the custard. Transfer to a freezer container and freeze the mixture for 1–2 hours until frozen 1 inch from the sides. Scrape into a bowl and beat again until smooth. Re-freeze until firm.

3 To make the cups, beat the egg white and sugar together. Beat in the flour and cocoa, then the butter. Place 1 tbsp of mixture on one sheet and spread out to a 5-inch round. Bake in a preheated oven at 400°F for 4–5 minutes. Remove and mold over an upturned cup. Let set, then cool on a wire rack. Repeat to make 6 cups. Serve the ice cream in the cookie cups.

Chocolate Horns with Ginger Cardamom Cream

Serves 6

INGREDIENTS

1 egg white	CARDAMOM CREAM:	pinch of ground ginger
4 tbsp superfine sugar	$2/3$ cup heavy cream	1 ounce preserved ginger, finely
2 tbsp all-purpose flour	1 tbsp confectioners' sugar	chopped
2 tbsp unsweetened cocoa	$1/4$ tsp ground cardamom	
2 tbsp butter, melted		
$1^3/4$ ounces dark chocolate		

1 Place a sheet of baking parchment on 2 cookie sheets. Lightly grease 6 cream horn molds. To make the horns, beat the egg white and sugar together in a mixing bowl until well combined. Sift the flour and unsweetened cocoa together, then beat into the egg, followed by the melted butter.

2 Place 1 tablespoon of the mixture on 1 cookie sheet and spread out to form a 5-inch round.

Bake in a preheated oven at 400°F for 4–5 minutes.

3 Working quickly, remove the cookie with a spatula and wrap around the cream horn mold to form a cone. Allow to set, then remove from the mold. Repeat to make 6 cones.

4 Melt the chocolate and dip the open edges of the horn in the chocolate. Place on a piece of baking parchment and allow to set.

5 To make the cardamom cream, place the cream in a bowl and sift the confectioners' sugar and ground spices over the surface. Whip the cream until standing in soft peaks. Fold in the chopped ginger and use to fill the chocolate cones.

Chocolate Charlotte

Serves 8

INGREDIENTS

about 22 ladyfingers

4 tbsp orange-flavored liqueur

9 ounces dark chocolate

²/₃ cup heavy cream

4 eggs

²/₃ cup superfine sugar

TO DECORATE:

²/₃ cup heavy cream

2 tbsp superfine sugar

¹/₂ tsp vanilla extract

large dark chocolate curls,
   chocolate leaves or chocolate
   shapes

1 Line the base of
a Charlotte mold or
a deep 7-inch round cake
pan with a piece of baking
parchment.

2 Place the ladyfingers
on a tray and sprinkle
with half the orange-
flavored liqueur. Use to line
the sides of the mold or
pan, trimming if necessary
to make a tight fit.

3 Break the chocolate
into small pieces and
melt in a double boiler.
Remove from the heat

and stir in the heavy cream
until well combined.

4 Separate the eggs
and place the whites
in a large grease-free bowl.
Beat the egg yolks into
the chocolate mixture.

5 Beat the egg whites
until standing in
stiff peaks, then gradually
add the superfine sugar,
beating until stiff and
glossy. Carefully fold
the egg whites into
the chocolate mixture
in 2 batches, taking care

not to knock out all the air.
Pour into the center
of the mold. Trim the
lady-fingers so that they
are level with the chocolate
mixture. Chill for at
least 5 hours.

6 To decorate, beat
the cream, sugar,
and vanilla extract together
until standing in soft peaks.
Turn out the Charlotte
onto a serving dish.
Pipe cream rosettes
around the base and
decorate with chocolate
curls and leaves.

Marble Cheesecake

Serves 10–12

INGREDIENTS

BASE:

2 cups toasted oatmeal

$1/2$ cup toasted hazelnuts, chopped

4 tbsp butter

1 ounce dark chocolate

FILLING:

12 ounces cream cheese

7 tbsp superfine sugar

$3/4$ cup thick unsweetened yogurt

$1 1/4$ cups heavy cream

1 envelope gelatin

3 tbsp water

6 ounces dark chocolate, melted

6 ounces white chocolate, melted

1 Place the toasted oatmeal in a plastic bag and crush with a rolling pin. Pour the crushed cereal into a mixing bowl and stir in the hazelnuts.

2 Melt the butter and chocolate together over a low heat and stir into the cereal mixture, stirring until well coated.

3 Using the bottom of a glass, press the mixture into the base and up the sides of an 8-inch springform pan.

4 Beat together the cheese and sugar with a wooden spoon until smooth. Beat in the yogurt. Whip the cream until just holding its shape and fold into the mixture. Sprinkle the gelatin over the water in a heatproof bowl and allow to become spongy. Place over a pan of hot water and stir until dissolved. Stir into the mixture.

5 Divide the mixture in half and beat the dark chocolate into one half and the white chocolate into the other half.

6 Place alternate spoonfuls of mixtures on top of the cereal base. Swirl the filling together with the tip of a knife to give a marbled effect. Level the top with a spatula. Chill in the refrigerator until set.

COOK'S TIP

For a lighter texture, fold in 2 egg whites beaten to soft peaks before folding in the cream in step 4.

Banana & Coconut Cheesecake

Serves 10

INGREDIENTS

8 ounces chocolate chip cookies	2 ripe bananas	TO DECORATE:
4 tbsp butter	4¹/₂ ounces dark chocolate	1 banana
1¹/₂ cups cream cheese	1 envelope gelatin	lemon juice
¹/₃ cup superfine sugar	3 tbsp water	a little melted chocolate
¹/₂ cup grated fresh coconut	²/₃ cup heavy cream	
2 tbsp coconut-flavored liqueur		

1 Place the cookies in a plastic bag and crush with a rolling pin. Pour into a mixing bowl. Melt the butter and stir it into the cookie crumbs until well coated. Firmly press the cookie mixture into the base and up the sides of an 8-inch springform pan.

2 Beat together the cheese and superfine sugar until well combined, then beat in the grated coconut and coconut-flavored liqueur. Mash the 2 bananas and beat them into the cheese mixture. Melt the dark chocolate and beat it in until well combined.

3 Sprinkle the gelatin over the water in a heatproof bowl and allow to become spongy. Place over a pan of hot water and stir until dissolved. Stir into the chocolate mixture. Whip the cream until just holding its shape and stir it into the chocolate mixture. Spoon over the cookie base and chill until set.

4 To serve, carefully transfer to a serving plate. Slice the banana, toss in the lemon juice, and arrange around the edge of the cheesecake. Drizzle with melted chocolate and allow to set.

COOK'S TIP

To crack the coconut, pierce 2 of the "eyes" and drain off the liquid. Tap hard around the center with a hammer until it cracks; split apart.

Chocolate Brandy Torte

Serves 12

INGREDIENTS

BASE:

9 ounces ginger cookies

2³/₄ ounces dark chocolate

¹/₂ cup butter

FILLING:

8 ounces dark chocolate

1¹/₄ cups mascarpone cheese

2 eggs, separated

3 tbsp brandy

1¹/₄ cups heavy cream

4 tbsp superfine sugar

TO DECORATE:

¹/₂ cup heavy cream

chocolate coffee beans

1 Put the cookies in a plastic bag and crush with a rolling pin or crush in a food processor. Transfer to a bowl. Melt the chocolate and butter together and pour over the cookies. Mix well, then use to line the base and sides of a 9-inch loose-based fluted flan pan or springform pan. Chill while you are preparing the filling.

2 To make the filling, melt the dark chocolate in a pan, remove from the heat, and beat in the mascarpone cheese, egg yolks, and brandy.

3 Lightly whip the cream until just holding its shape and fold in the chocolate mixture.

4 Beat the egg whites in a grease-free bowl until standing in soft peaks. Add the superfine sugar a little at a time and beat until thick and glossy. Fold into the chocolate mixture, in 2 batches, until just mixed.

5 Spoon the mixture into the prepared base and chill for at least 2 hours. Carefully transfer to a serving plate. To decorate, whip the cream and pipe onto the cheesecake and add the chocolate coffee beans.

VARIATION

If chocolate coffee beans are unavailable, use chocolate-coated raisins to decorate.

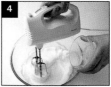

Chocolate Shortcake Towers

Serves 6

INGREDIENTS

SHORTCAKE:
1 cup butter
$^1/_2$ cup light brown sugar
$1^3/_4$ ounces dark chocolate, grated
$2^1/_2$ cups all-purpose flour

TO FINISH:
2 cups fresh raspberries
2 tbsp confectioners' sugar
$1^1/_4$ cups heavy cream
3 tbsp milk

3 ounces white chocolate, melted
confectioners' sugar, to dust

1 Lightly grease a cookie sheet. To make the shortcake, beat together the butter and sugar until light and fluffy. Beat in the dark chocolate. Mix in the flour to form a stiff dough.

2 Roll out the dough on a lightly floured surface and stamp out eighteen 3-inch rounds with a fluted cookie cutter. Place the rounds on the cookie sheet and bake in a preheated oven at 400°F for 10 minutes, until crisp and golden. Cool on the cookie sheet.

3 To make the coulis, set aside about $^1/_2$ cup of the raspberries. Put the remainder in a food processor together with the confectioners' sugar, and process to a purée. Rub through a strainer to remove the seeds. Chill. Set aside 2 teaspoons of the cream. Whip the remainder until just holding its shape. Fold in the milk and the melted chocolate.

4 For each tower, spoon a little coulis onto a serving plate. Drop small dots of the reserved cream into the coulis around the edge of the plate and use a toothpick to drag through the cream to make a pattern.

5 Place a shortcake round on the plate and spoon on a little of the chocolate cream. Top with 2 or 3 raspberries, top with another shortcake and repeat. Place a third cake on top. Dust with sugar.

Black Forest Trifle

Serves 6–8

INGREDIENTS

6 thin slices chocolate butter cream roll	1¾ cups milk	TO DECORATE:
2 x 14 ounce cans black cherries	3 egg yolks	dark chocolate, melted
2 tbsp kirsch	1 egg	maraschino cherries (optional)
1 tbsp cornstarch	2¾ ounces dark chocolate	
2 tbsp superfine sugar	1¼ cups heavy cream, lightly whipped	

1 Place the slices of chocolate roll in the bottom of a glass serving bowl.

2 Drain the black cherries, reserving 6 tablespoons of the juice. Arrange the cherries on top of the layer of cake. Sprinkle with the reserved cherry juice and the kirsch.

3 In a bowl, mix the cornstarch and super-fine sugar. Stir in enough of the milk to mix to a smooth paste. Beat in the egg yolks and the whole egg.

4 Heat the remaining milk in a small saucepan until almost boiling, then gradually pour it into the egg mixture, beating well until it is combined.

5 Place the bowl over a pan of hot water and cook over a low heat, stirring constantly, until the custard thickens. Add the chocolate and stir until melted.

6 Pour the chocolate custard over the cherries and cool. When cold, spread the cream over the custard, swirling with the back of a spoon. Chill before decorating.

7 To make chocolate caraque, spread the melted dark chocolate on a marble or acrylic board. As it begins to set, pull a knife through the chocolate at a 45-degree angle, working quickly. Remove each caraque as you make it and chill firmly before using.

Champagne Mousse

Serves 4

INGREDIENTS

SPONGE:

4 eggs

7 tbsp superfine sugar

²/₃ cup self-rising flour

2 tbsp unsweetened cocoa

2 tbsp butter, melted

MOUSSE:

1 envelope gelatin

3 tbsp water

1¼ cups Champagne

1¼ cups heavy cream

2 egg whites

¹/₃ cup superfine sugar

TO DECORATE:

2 ounces dark chocolate, melted

fresh strawberries

1 Line a 15 x 10 inch jelly roll pan with greased baking parchment. Place the eggs and sugar in a bowl and beat with an electric mixer until the mixture is very thick and the beater leaves a trail when lifted. Sift the flour and unsweetened cocoa together and fold into the egg mixture. Fold in the butter. Pour into the pan and bake in a preheated oven at 400°F for 8 minutes, or until springy to the touch. Cool for 5 minutes, then turn out onto a wire rack until cold. Line four 4-inch

baking rings with baking parchment. Line the sides with 1-inch strips of cake and the bases with rounds.

2 To make the mousse, sprinkle the gelatin over the water and set aside until it is spongy. Place the bowl over a pan of hot water; stir until completely dissolved. Stir in the champagne.

3 Whip the cream until just holding its shape. Fold in the champagne mixture. Leave in a cool

place, stirring occasionally, until on the point of setting. Beat the egg whites until the mixture stands in soft peaks, add the sugar and beat until glossy. Fold into the setting mixture. Spoon into the sponge cases, allowing the mixture to go above the sponge. Chill in the refrigerator for 2 hours. Pipe the melted chocolate in squiggles on a piece of parchment and let set. Decorate the mousses.

Chocolate Freezer Cake

Serves 8–10

INGREDIENTS

4 eggs

¾ cup superfine sugar

¾ cup self-rising flour

3 tbsp unsweetened cocoa

2¼ cups chocolate and mint
    ice cream

Glossy Chocolate Sauce

1 Lightly grease a 9-inch ring pan. Place the eggs and sugar in a large mixing bowl. Using an electric mixer if you have one, beat the mixture until it is very thick and the beater leaves a trail when lifted.

2 Sift together the flour and unsweetened cocoa and fold into the egg mixture. Pour into the prepared pan and bake in a preheated oven at 350°F for 30 minutes, or until springy to the touch. Cool in the pan before turning out onto a wire rack to cool completely.

3 Rinse the cake pan and line with a strip of plastic wrap, overhanging slightly. Cut the top off the cake about ½ inch thick and set aside.

4 Return the cake to the pan. Using a spoon, scoop out the center of the cake, leaving a shell about ½ inch thick.

5 Remove the ice cream from the freezer and let stand for a few minutes, then beat with a wooden spoon until softened a little. Fill the center of the cake with the ice cream, leveling the top. Replace the top of the cake.

6 Cover with the overhanging plastic wrap and freeze for at least 2 hours.

7 To serve, turn the cake out onto a serving dish and drizzle with some of the chocolate sauce in an attractive pattern, if you wish. Cut the cake into slices and serve the remaining sauce separately.

Mississippi Mud Pie

Serves 8–10

INGREDIENTS

2 cups all-purpose flour
$\frac{1}{4}$ cup unsweetened cocoa
$\frac{2}{3}$ cup butter
5 tsp superfine sugar
about 2 tbsp cold water

FILLING:
$\frac{3}{4}$ cup butter
12 ounces dark brown sugar
4 eggs, lightly beaten
4 tbsp unsweetened cocoa, sifted
$5\frac{1}{2}$ ounces dark chocolate
$1\frac{1}{4}$ cups light cream

1 tsp chocolate extract

TO DECORATE:
$1\frac{3}{4}$ cups heavy cream, whipped
thick bar of chocolate

1 To make the dough, sift the flour and unsweetened cocoa together into a mixing bowl. Rub in the butter with your fingertips until the mixture resembles fine breadcrumbs. Stir in the sugar and just enough cold water to mix to a soft dough. Chill for about 15 minutes.

2 Roll out the dough on a lightly floured surface and use to line a deep 9-inch loose-based flan pan or ceramic flan dish. Line with foil or baking parchment and dried beans. Bake in a preheated oven at 375°F for 15 minutes. Remove the beans and foil or paper and cook for a further 10 minutes, until crisp.

3 To make the filling, beat the butter and sugar in a bowl and gradually beat in the eggs with the unsweetened cocoa. Melt the chocolate and beat it into the mixture with the light cream and the chocolate extract.

4 Pour the mixture into the cooked pie shell and bake at 325°F for 45 minutes, or until the filling is set.

5 Let cool completely, then transfer the pie to a serving plate, if desired. Cover with the whipped cream and chill.

6 To make small chocolate curls, use a peeler to remove curls from the bar of chocolate. Decorate the pie and chill.

Chocolate Fruit Tartlets

Serves 6

INGREDIENTS

1¼ cups all-purpose flour	2–3 tbsp water	3 tbsp apricot preserve or red
3 tbsp unsweetened cocoa	1¾ ounces dark chocolate	currant jelly
⅔ cup butter	½ cup chopped mixed nuts, toasted	
3 tbsp superfine sugar	12 ounces prepared fruit	

1 Sift together the flour and unsweetened cocoa into a mixing bowl. Cut the butter into small pieces and rub it into the flour with your fingertips until the mixture resembles fine breadcrumbs.

2 Stir in the sugar. Add just enough of the water to mix to a soft dough, approximately 1–2 tablespoons. Cover and chill in the refrigerator for about 15 minutes.

3 Roll out the dough on a lightly floured surface and use to line six 4-inch tartlet pans.

Prick the dough with a fork and line the pie shells with a little crumpled foil. Bake in a preheated oven at 375°F for 10 minutes.

4 Remove the foil and bake for a further 5–10 minutes, until the pastry is crisp. Place the pans on a wire rack to cool completely.

5 Melt the chocolate. Spread out the chopped nuts on a plate. Remove the pie shells from the tins pans. Spread melted chocolate on the rims, then dip in the nuts. Let set.

6 Arrange the fruit in the tartlet shells. Melt the apricot preserve or red currant jelly with the remaining 1 tablespoon of water and brush it over the fruit. Chill the tartlets until required.

VARIATION

If desired, you can fill the cases with a little sweetened cream before topping with the fruit. For a chocolate-flavored filling, blend 8 ounces chocolate hazelnut spread with 5 tablespoons of thick yogurt or whipped cream.

Banana Cream Puffs

Serves 4-6

INGREDIENTS

CHOUX PASTRY:
²/₃ cup water
¹/₄ cup butter
³/₄ cup strong all-purpose
flour, sifted
2 eggs

CHOCOLATE SAUCE:
3¹/₂ ounces dark chocolate, broken
into pieces
2 tbsp water
4 tbsp confectioners' sugar
2 tbsp sweet butter

FILLING:
1¹/₄ cups heavy cream
1 banana
2 tbsp confectioners' sugar
2 tbsp banana-flavored liqueur

1 Lightly grease a cookie sheet and sprinkle with a little water. To make the pastry, place the water in a pan. Cut the butter into small pieces and add to the pan. Heat gently until the butter melts, then bring to a rolling boil. Remove the pan from the heat and add the flour all at once, beating well until the mixture leaves the sides of the pan and forms a ball. Let cool slightly, then gradually beat in the eggs to form a smooth, glossy mixture. Spoon the paste into a large pastry bag fitted with a ¹/₂-inch plain tip.

2 Pipe about 18 small balls of the paste onto the prepared cookie sheet, allowing enough room for them to expand during cooking. Bake in a preheated oven at 425°F for 15–20 minutes, until crisp and golden. Remove from the oven and make a small slit in each one for the steam to escape. Transfer to a wire rack and let cool completely.

3 To make the sauce, heat all the ingredients in a double boiler, stirring until combined to make a smooth sauce.

4 To make the filling, whip the cream until standing in soft peaks. Using a fork, mash the banana with the sugar and liqueur. Fold into the cream. Place the filling in a pastry bag fitted with a ¹/₂-inch plain tip and pipe into the cream puffs. Serve with the sauce poured on top.

Chocolate Mousse

Serves 8

INGREDIENTS

3¹/₂ ounces dark chocolate, melted
1¹/₄ cups plain yogurt
²/₃ cup cream cheese
4 tablespoons sugar

1 tablespoon orange juice
1 tablespoon brandy
1¹/₂ teaspoons agar*
9 tablespoons cold water

2 large egg whites
coarsely grated dark and white
    chocolate and orange zest,
    to decorate

1 Put the chocolate, yogurt, cream cheese, sugar, orange juice and brandy in a food processor and process for 30 seconds. Transfer the mixture to a large bowl.

2 Sprinkle the agar over the water and stir until completely dissolved.

3 In a small pan, bring the agar and water to a boil for 2 minutes. Set aside to cool slightly, then stir into the chocolate mixture.

4 Whisk the egg whites until stiff peaks form, then fold them into the chocolate mixture using a metal spoon.

5 Line a 4-cup loaf pan with plastic wrap. Spoon the mousse into it. Chill for 2 hours in the refrigerator, until set. Turn the mousse out onto a serving plate, decorate with chocolate and orange zest, and serve.

COOK'S TIP

For a quick fruit sauce, process a can of mandarin segments in natural juice in a food processor and press through a strainer. Stir in 1 tablespoon honey and serve with the mousse.

Tiramisu

Serves 6

INGREDIENTS

10¹/₂ ounces dark chocolate
1³/₄ cups mascarpone cheese
²/₃ cup heavy cream, whipped until
it just holds its shape

1³/₄ cups black coffee with
¹/₄ cup superfine sugar, cooled
6 tbsp dark rum or brandy

36 lady fingers, about 14 oz
unsweetened cocoa, to dust

1 Melt the chocolate in a bowl set over a saucepan of simmering water, stirring occasionally. Leave the chocolate to cool slightly, then stir it into the mascarpone and cream.

2 Mix the coffee and rum together in a bowl. Dip the lady fingers into the mixture briefly so that they absorb the liquid, but do not become soggy and disintegrate.

3 Place 3 lady fingers on 3 serving plates.

4 Spoon a layer of the mascarpone and chocolate mixture over the lady fingers.

5 Place 3 more lady fingers on top of the mascarpone layer. Spread another layer of mascarpone and chocolate mixture and place 3 more lady fingers on top.

6 Chill the tiramisu in the refrigerator for at least 1 hour. Dust with a little unsweetened cocoa just before serving.

COOK'S TIP

Tiramisu can also be served semi-frozen, like ice cream. Freeze the tiramisu for 2 hours and serve immediately, as it defrosts very quickly.

VARIATION

Try adding ¹/₂ cup toasted, chopped hazelnuts to the chocolate cream mixture in step 1, if desired.

Rich Chocolate Loaf

Makes 16 Slices

INGREDIENTS

5¹/₂ ounces dark chocolate	2 tsp cinnamon	¹/₄ cup chopped dried no-need-to-soak apricots
6 tbsp sweet butter	¹/₂ cup almonds,	
7¹/₄ ounce can condensed milk	1 cup broken amaretti cookies	

1 Line a 1¹/₂-pound loaf pan with a sheet of foil.

2 Using a very sharp knife, roughly chop the almonds.

3 Place the chocolate, butter, milk, and cinnamon in a heavy-based saucepan. Heat gently over a low heat for 3–4 minutes, stirring with a wooden spoon, until the chocolate has melted. Beat the mixture well.

4 Add the almonds, cookies, and apricots to the mixture in the saucepan, stirring with a wooden spoon, until well mixed.

5 Pour the mixture into the prepared pan and chill in the refrigerator for about 1 hour, or until set.

6 Cut the rich chocolate loaf into slices to serve.

COOK'S TIP

To melt chocolate, first break it into manageable pieces. The smaller the pieces, the quicker it will melt.

COOK'S TIP

When baking or cooking with fat, butter has the finest flavor. If possible, it is best to use sweet butter as an ingredient in puddings and desserts, unless stated otherwise in the recipe. Reduced fat spreads are not suitable for cooking.

Chocolate & Bean Curd Cheesecake

Serves 12

INGREDIENTS

³/₄ cup all-purpose flour
³/₄ cup ground almonds
³/₄ cup raw brown crystal sugar
10 tablespoons vegetarian
    margarine

1¹/₂ pounds firm bean curd
³/₄ cup vegetable oil
¹/₂ cup orange juice
³/₄ cup brandy

6 tablespoons unsweetened cocoa,
    plus extra to decorate
2 teaspoons almond extract
confectioners' sugar and Cape
    gooseberries, to decorate

1 Put the flour, ground almonds, and 1 tablespoon of the sugar in a bowl and mix well. Rub the margarine into the mixture with the fingertips to form a dough.

2 Lightly grease and line the base of a 9-inch springform pan. Press the dough into the base of the pan to cover, pushing the dough right up to the edge.

3 Roughly chop the bean curd and put it in a food processor, together with all of the remaining ingredients, and process until smooth and creamy. Pour the purée over the base in the pan and cook in a preheated oven at 325°F for 1–1¹/₄ hours, or until set.

4 Let cool in the pan for 5 minutes, then remove from the pan and chill in the refrigerator. Dust with confectioners' sugar and unsweetened cocoa. Decorate with cape gooseberries and serve.

Eve's Pudding

Serves 6

INGREDIENTS

1 pound cooking apples, peeled,
   cored, and sliced
$\frac{1}{3}$ cup granulated sugar
1 tbsp lemon juice

$\frac{1}{3}$ cup golden raisins
$\frac{1}{3}$ cup butter
$\frac{1}{3}$ cup superfine sugar
1 egg, beaten

$1\frac{1}{4}$ cups self-rising flour
3 tbsp milk
$\frac{1}{4}$ cup slivered almonds
custard or heavy cream,
   to serve

1 Thoroughly grease a
$3\frac{1}{2}$ cup ovenproof dish.

2 Mix the apples with
the sugar, lemon juice,
and golden raisins. Spoon
the mixture into the dish.

3 In a bowl, cream the
butter and superfine
sugar together until pale.
Add the egg, a little at a time.

4 Carefully fold in
the self-rising flour and
stir in the milk to give a
soft, dropping consistency.

5 Spread the mixture over
the apples and sprinkle
with the slivered almonds.

6 Bake in a preheated
oven at 350°F for
40–45 minutes, until
the sponge is a light golden
brown color.

7 Serve the pudding
hot, with custard or
heavy cream.

COOK'S TIP

*To increase the almond
flavor of this apple
pudding, add $\frac{1}{4}$ cup
ground almonds with
the flour in step 4.*

Queen of Puddings

Serves 8

INGREDIENTS

2½ cups milk
2 tbsp butter
1¼ cups superfine sugar

finely grated rind of 1 orange
4 eggs, separated
¾ cup fresh breadcrumbs

pinch of salt
6 tbsp orange marmalade

1 Thoroughly grease a 6 cup ovenproof dish.

2 To make the custard, heat the milk in a pan with the butter, ¼ cup of the superfine sugar, and the grated orange rind until just warm.

3 Whisk the egg yolks in a bowl. Gradually pour the warm milk over the eggs, stirring.

4 Stir the breadcrumbs into the pan, then transfer the mixture to the prepared dish, and let stand for 15 minutes.

5 Bake in a preheated oven at 350°F for 20–25 minutes, until the custard has just set. Remove the custard from the oven, but do not turn the oven off.

6 To make the meringue, whisk the egg whites with a pinch of salt until they stand in soft peaks. Whisk in the remaining sugar, a little at a time.

7 Spread the orange marmalade over the cooked custard. Top with the meringue, spreading it to the edges of the dish.

8 Return the pudding to the oven and bake for a further 20 minutes, until the meringue is crisp and golden.

Bread & Butter Pudding

Serves 6

INGREDIENTS

7 ounces white bread, sliced	2 tbsp golden raisins	4 egg yolks
4 tbsp butter, softened	$\frac{1}{8}$ cup candied peel	$\frac{1}{3}$ cup superfine sugar
	$2\frac{1}{2}$ cups milk	$\frac{1}{2}$ tsp apple pie spice

1 Grease a $5\frac{1}{3}$ cup ovenproof dish.

2 Remove the crusts from the bread (optional). Spread with the butter and cut the slices in half.

3 Arrange half of the buttered bread slices in the prepared ovenproof dish. Sprinkle half of the golden raisins and candied peel over the top of the bread.

4 Place the remaining bread slices over the fruit, and then top with the reserved fruit.

5 To make the custard, bring the milk almost to a boil in a saucepan. Whisk together the egg yolks and the sugar in a bowl, then pour in the warm milk.

6 Pour the warm custard through a strainer. Then pour the custard over the bread slices.

7 Let stand for 30 minutes, then sprinkle with the apple pie spice.

8 Place the ovenproof dish in a roasting pan half-filled with hot water.

9 Bake in a preheated oven at 400°F for 40–45 minutes, until the pudding has just set. Serve warm.

Plum Cobbler

Serves 6

INGREDIENTS

2¼ pounds plums, pits removed,
and sliced
⅓ cup superfine sugar
1 tbsp lemon juice

2¼ cups all-purpose flour
⅓ cup granulated sugar
2 tsp baking powder
1 egg, beaten

⅔ cup buttermilk
6 tbsp butter, melted and cooled
heavy cream, to serve

1 Lightly grease an 8 cup ovenproof dish.

2 In a large bowl, mix together the plums, superfine sugar, lemon juice, and ¼ cup of the all-purpose flour.

3 Spoon the coated plums into the bottom of the ovenproof dish.

4 Mix together the remaining flour, granulated sugar, and baking powder in a bowl until well combined.

5 Add the beaten egg, buttermilk, and cooled melted butter. Mix together to form a soft dough.

6 Place spoonfuls of the dough on top of the fruit mixture until it is almost covered.

7 Bake the cobbler in a preheated oven at 375°F for about 35–40 minutes, until golden brown and bubbling.

8 Serve the pudding hot, with heavy cream.

COOK'S TIP

If you cannot find buttermilk, try using sour cream.

Blackberry Pudding

Serves 4

INGREDIENTS

1 pound blackberries
⅓ cup superfine sugar
1 egg
⅓ cup light brown sugar

6 tbsp butter, melted
8 tbsp milk
1 cup self-rising flour

1 Lightly grease a large 3½ cup ovenproof dish.

2 In a large mixing bowl, gently mix together the blackberries and superfine sugar until they are thoroughly combined.

3 Transfer the blackberry and sugar mixture to the prepared ovenproof dish.

4 Beat together the egg and light brown sugar in a mixing bowl until well combined. Stir in the melted butter and milk.

5 Sift the flour into the egg and butter mixture and fold together lightly to form a smooth batter.

6 Carefully spread the batter over the blackberry and sugar mixture in the dish, to cover the fruit.

7 Bake the pudding in a preheated oven at 350°F for 25–30 minutes, until the topping is firm and golden.

8 Sprinkle the pudding with a little sugar, if desired, and serve hot.

VARIATION

You can add 2 tablespoons of unsweetened cocoa to the batter in step 5, if you prefer a chocolate flavor.

Raspberry Shortcake

Serves 8

INGREDIENTS

1 ½ cups self-rising flour
7 tbsp butter, cut into cubes
⅓ cup superfine sugar
1 egg yolk
1 tbsp rose water

2 ½ cups whipping cream,
  whipped lightly
1⅓ cups raspberries, plus a few for
  decoration

TO DECORATE:
confectioners' sugar
mint leaves

1 Lightly grease
2 cookie sheets.

2 To make the
shortcakes, sift
the flour into a bowl.

3 Rub the butter into
the flour with your
fingers until the mixture
resembles breadcrumbs.

4 Stir the sugar, egg
yolk, and rose water
into the mixture and bring
together with your fingertips
to form a soft dough.
Divide the dough in half.

5 Roll each piece of
dough to an 8-inch
round and place each one
onto a prepared cookie
sheet. Crimp the edges of
the dough.

6 Bake in a preheated
oven at 375°F for
15 minutes, until lightly
golden. Transfer the
shortcakes to a wire rack
and let cool.

7 Mix the cream
with the raspberries
and spoon on top of one
of the shortcake rounds.

Top with the other
shortcake round, dust
with a little confectioners'
sugar, and decorate with
the extra raspberries
and mint leaves.

COOK'S TIP

*The shortcake can be made
a few days in advance and
stored in an airtight
container until required.*

Pavlova

Serves 6

INGREDIENTS

3 egg whites
pinch of salt
¾ cup superfine sugar

1 ¼ cups heavy cream, lightly
  whipped

fresh fruit of your choice
  (raspberries, strawberries,
  peaches, passion fruit, ground
  cherries)

1 Line a large cookie sheet with a sheet of baking parchment.

2 Whisk the egg whites with the salt in a bowl until they form soft peaks.

3 Whisk in the sugar a little at a time, whisking well after each addition.

4 Spoon three-quarters of the meringue onto the cookie sheet, forming a round 8 inches in diameter.

5 Place spoonfuls of the remaining meringue all around the edge of the round so they join up to make a nest shape.

6 Bake in a preheated oven at 275°F for 1¼ hours.

7 Turn the heat off, but leave the pavlova in the oven until it is completely cold.

8 To serve, transfer the pavlova to a serving dish. Gently spread with the lightly whipped heavy cream, then arrange the fresh fruit on top.

COOK'S TIP

It is a good idea to make the pavlova in the evening and leave it in the turned-off oven overnight.

Sticky Chocolate Pudding

Serves 6

INGREDIENTS

$^1/_2$ cup butter, softened
$^3/_4$ cup light brown sugar
3 eggs, beaten
pinch of salt
$^1/_4$ cup unsweetened cocoa

1 cup self-rising flour
1 ounce dark chocolate,
    finely chopped
2$^3/_4$ ounces white chocolate,
    finely chopped

SAUCE:
$^2/_3$ cup heavy cream
$^1/_3$ cup light brown sugar
2 tbsp butter

1 Lightly grease 6 individual $^3/_4$ cup pudding molds.

2 Cream together the butter and sugar until pale and fluffy. Beat in the eggs, a little at a time.

3 Sift the salt, unsweetened cocoa, and flour into the creamed mixture and fold through the mixture. Stir the chopped chocolate into the mixture until evenly combined.

4 Divide the mixture between the prepared pudding molds. Lightly grease 6 squares of foil and use them to cover the tops of the molds. Press around the edges to seal.

5 Place the molds in a roasting pan and pour in boiling water to come halfway up the sides of the molds.

6 Bake in a preheated oven at 350°F for 50 minutes, or until

a toothpick inserted into the center comes out clean. Remove the molds from the roasting pan and set aside.

7 To make the sauce, put the cream, sugar, and butter into a pan and bring to a boil over a gentle heat. Simmer gently until the sugar has dissolved.

8 Turn the puddings out onto individual serving plates. Pour the sauce over the top of the puddings and serve.

Chocolate Brownie Roulade

Serves 8

INGREDIENTS

5 ½ ounces dark chocolate, broken
    into pieces
3 tbsp water
¾ cup superfine sugar

5 eggs, separated
2 tbsp raisins, chopped
¼ cup chopped pecans
pinch of salt

1 ¼ cups heavy cream,
    whipped lightly
confectioners' sugar, for dusting

1 Grease a 12 × 8-inch jelly roll pan and line with greased baking parchment.

2 Heat the chocolate with the water in a small saucepan over a low heat until the chocolate has just melted. Let cool.

3 Whisk the sugar and egg yolks for about 2–3 minutes until thick. Fold in the chocolate, raisins, and pecans.

4 Whisk the egg whites with the salt. Fold one-quarter of the egg whites into the chocolate mixture, then lightly fold in the rest.

5 Transfer the mixture to the prepared pan and bake in a preheated oven at 350°F for 25 minutes, until risen and just firm to the touch. Remove from the oven and let cool before covering with a sheet of nonstick baking parchment and a damp clean dish cloth. Leave until completely cold.

6 Turn the roulade out onto another piece of baking parchment dusted with confectioners' sugar and remove the lining paper.

7 Spread the whipped heavy cream over the roulade. Starting from a short end, roll the sponge away from you using the paper to guide you. Trim the ends of the roulade to make a neat finish and transfer to a serving plate. Chill in the refrigerator until ready to serve. Dust with a little confectioners' sugar before serving, if desired.

One Roll Fruit Pie

Serves 8

INGREDIENTS

PIE DOUGH:

$1\frac{1}{2}$ cups all-purpose flour

7 tbsp butter, cut into
    small pieces

1 tbsp water

1 egg, separated

sugar cubes, crushed, for sprinkling

FILLING:

$1\frac{1}{2}$ pound prepared fruit (rhubarb,
    gooseberries, plums, damsons)

6 tbsp light brown sugar

1 tbsp ground ginger

1 Thoroughly grease a large cookie sheet with a little butter.

2 To make the pie dough, place the flour and butter in a mixing bowl and rub in the butter with your fingers. Add the water and work the mixture together until a soft pie dough has formed. Wrap and chill for 30 minutes.

3 Roll out the chilled pie dough to a round measuring about 14 inches in diameter.

4 Transfer the round to the center of the greased cookie sheet. Brush the pie dough with the egg yolk.

5 To make the filling, mix the prepared fruit with the brown sugar and ground ginger and pile it into the center of the pie dough.

6 Turn in the edges of the pie dough all the way around. Brush the surface of the pie dough with the egg white and sprinkle evenly with the crushed sugar cubes.

7 Bake in a preheated oven at 400°F for 35 minutes, or until golden brown. Serve warm.

Fruit Crumble Tart

Serves 8

INGREDIENTS

PIE DOUGH:

1¼ cups all-purpose flour

5 tsp superfine sugar

9 tbsp butter, cut into small pieces

1 tbsp water

FILLING:

1½ cups raspberries

1 pound plums, halved, pitted, and
    roughly chopped

3 tbsp raw crystal sugar

TO SERVE:

light cream

TOPPING:

1 cup all-purpose flour

⅓ cup raw crystal sugar

⅓ cup butter, cut into small pieces

1 cup chopped mixed nuts

1 tsp ground cinnamon

1 To make the pie dough, place the flour, sugar, and butter in a bowl and rub in the butter with your fingers. Add the water and work the mixture together until a soft pie dough has formed. Wrap and chill for 30 minutes.

2 Roll out the pie dough to line the base of a 10-inch loose-bottomed quiche pan. Prick the base of the pie dough with a fork and chill for about 30 minutes.

3 To make the filling, toss the raspberries and plums together with the sugar and spoon into the pie shell.

4 To make the crumble topping, combine the flour, sugar, and butter in a bowl. Work the butter into the flour with your fingers until the mixture resembles coarse breadcrumbs. Stir in the nuts and ground cinnamon.

5 Sprinkle the topping over the fruit and bake in a preheated oven at 400°F for 20–25 minutes, until the topping is golden. Serve with light cream.

Cheese & Apple Tart

Serves 8

INGREDIENTS

1 ½ cups self-rising flour	¾ cup pitted dates, chopped	¼ cup sunflower oil
1 tsp baking powder	1 pound 2 ounces eating apples,	2 eggs
pinch of salt	cored and chopped	1 ½ cups grated Red Leicester
⅓ cup light brown sugar	½ cup chopped walnuts	cheese

1 Grease a 10-inch loose-bottomed quiche pan with butter and line with baking parchment.

2 Sift the flour, baking powder, and salt into a bowl. Stir in the brown sugar and the chopped dates, apples, and walnuts. Thoroughly mix together until well combined.

3 Beat the oil and eggs together and add the mixture to the dry ingredients. Stir until thoroughly combined.

4 Spoon half of the mixture into the pan and level the surface.

5 Sprinkle with the cheese, then spoon over the remaining cake mixture, spreading it to the edges of the pan.

6 Bake in a preheated oven at 350°F for 45–50 minutes, or until golden brown and firm to the touch.

7 Cool slightly in the pan. Serve warm.

COOK'S TIP

This is a deliciously moist tart. Any leftovers should be stored in the refrigerator and heated to serve.

Apple Tart Tatin

Serves 8

INGREDIENTS

9 tbsp butter
$^1/_2$ cup superfine sugar
4 eating apples, cored and
    quartered

9 ounces fresh ready-made
    pie dough
crème fraîche, to serve

1 Heat the butter and sugar in a 9-inch ovenproof skillet over a medium heat for about 5 minutes, until the mixture begins to caramelize. Remove the skillet from the heat.

2 Arrange the apple quarters, skin side down, in the skillet, taking care as the butter and sugar are very hot. Place the skillet back on the heat and simmer for 2 minutes.

3 On a lightly floured surface, roll out the pie dough to form a round just larger than the skillet.

4 Place the pie dough over the apples, press down, and tuck in the edges to seal the apples under the layer of pie dough.

5 Bake in a preheated oven at 400°F for 20–25 minutes, until the pie dough is golden. Remove from the oven and let cool for 10 minutes.

6 Place a serving plate over the skillet and invert so that the pastry forms the base of the turned-out tart. Serve the tart warm with crème fraîche.

VARIATION

Replace the apples with pears, if you prefer. Leave the skin on the pears, cut them into quarters, and then remove the cores.

Syrup Tart

Serves 8

INGREDIENTS

9 ounces fresh ready-made
    shortcrust pie dough
1 cup light corn syrup
2 cups fresh white breadcrumbs
$\frac{1}{2}$ cup heavy cream

finely grated rind of $\frac{1}{2}$ lemon
    or orange
2 tbsp lemon or orange juice
custard, to serve

1 Roll out the pie dough to line an 8-inch loose-bottomed quiche pan, reserving the pie dough trimmings. Prick the base of the pie dough with a fork and chill in the refrigerator.

2 Cut out small shapes from the reserved pie dough trimmings, such as leaves, stars, or hearts, to decorate the top of the syrup tart.

3 In a mixing bowl, mix together the corn syrup, breadcrumbs, cream, grated lemon or orange rind, and lemon or orange juice.

4 Pour the mixture into the pie shell and decorate the edges of the tart with the pie dough cut-outs.

5 Bake in a preheated oven at 375°F for 35–40 minutes, or until the filling is just set.

6 Leave the tart to cool slightly in the pan for about 10–15 minutes, then turn out and serve the tart accompanied by custard.

VARIATION

Use the pie dough trimmings to create a lattice pattern on top of the tart, if preferred.

Apple & Mincemeat Tart

Serves 8

INGREDIENTS

pie dough:

1 ¼ cups all-purpose flour

2 tbsp superfine sugar

½ cup butter, cut into
    small pieces

1 tbsp water

FILLING:

14½ ounce jar mincemeat

3 eating apples, cored

1 tbsp lemon juice

6 tsp light corn syrup

3 tbsp butter

1 To make the pie dough, place the flour and superfine sugar in a large mixing bowl, add the butter, and rub in with your fingertips until the mixture resembles fine breadcrumbs.

2 Add the water and work the mixture together until a soft pie dough has formed. Wrap and chill in the refrigerator for 30 minutes.

3 On a lightly floured surface, roll out the dough and line

a 10-inch loose-bottomed quiche pan. Prick the dough with a fork and chill in the refrigerator for 30 minutes.

4 Line the pie shell with foil and dried beans. Bake the shell in a preheated oven at 375°F for 15 minutes. Remove the foil and beans and cook the shell for another 15 minutes.

5 Grate the apple and mix with the mincemeat and lemon

juice until well combined and spoon into the baked pie shell.

6 Melt the syrup and butter together and pour over the mincemeat mixture.

7 Return the tart to the oven for 20 minutes, until firm. Serve warm.

VARIATION

Add 2 tbsp sherry to spice up the mincemeat, if you wish.

Custard Tart

Serves 8

INGREDIENTS

PIE DOUGH;
1¼ cups all-purpose flour
5 tsp superfine sugar
²⁄₃ cup butter, cut into small pieces
1 tbsp water

FILLING:
3 eggs
²⁄₃ cup light cream
²⁄₃ cup milk
freshly grated nutmeg

TO SERVE:
whipped cream

1 To make the pie dough, place the flour and sugar in a mixing bowl and rub in the butter with your fingertips until the mixture resembles fine breadcrumbs.

2 Add the water and mix together until a soft pie dough has formed. Wrap and chill in the refrigerator for about 30 minutes.

3 Roll out the dough to form a round slightly larger than a 10-inch loose-bottomed quiche pan.

4 Line the pan with the dough, trimming off the edges. Prick the dough with a fork and chill in the refrigerator for 30 minutes.

5 Line the pie shell with a sheet of foil and dried beans.

6 Bake in a preheated oven at 375°F for 15 minutes. Remove the foil and beans and bake the pie shell for a further 15 minutes.

7 To make the filling, whisk together the eggs, cream, milk, and nutmeg. Pour the filling into the prepared pie shell. Transfer the tart to the oven and cook for about 25–30 minutes, or until just set. Serve with whipped cream, if desired.

Lemon Tart

Serves 8

INGREDIENTS

PIE DOUGH:
1 ¼ cups all-purpose flour
5 tsp superfine sugar
½ cup butter, cut into small pieces
1 tbsp water

FILLING:
⅔ cup heavy cream
½ cup superfine sugar
4 eggs
grated rind of 3 lemons

12 tbsp lemon juice
confectioners' sugar, for dusting

1 To make the pie dough, place the flour and sugar in a bowl and rub in the butter using your fingertips. Add the water and mix until a soft pie dough has formed. Wrap and chill for 30 minutes.

2 On a lightly floured surface, roll out the dough and line a 10-inch loose-bottomed quiche pan. Prick the pie dough all over with a fork and chill for 30 minutes.

3 Line the pie shell with foil and dried beans and bake blind in a preheated oven at 375°F for 15 minutes. Remove the foil and beans, return to the oven and cook the pie shell for another 15 minutes.

4 To make the filling, whisk the cream, sugar, eggs, and lemon rind and juice together. Place the pie shell, still in its pan, on a cookie sheet and pour in the filling.

5 Bake in the oven for about 20 minutes, or until just set. Let to cool, then lightly dust with confectioners' sugar before serving.

Orange Tart

Serves 6-8

INGREDIENTS

PIE DOUGH:

1 ¼ cups all-purpose flour

5 tsp superfine sugar

½ cup butter, cut into
   small pieces

1 tbsp water

FILLING:

grated rind of 2 oranges

9 tbsp orange juice

⅞ cups fresh white breadcrumbs

2 tbsp lemon juice

⅔ cup light cream

¼ cup butter

¼ cup superfine sugar

2 eggs, separated

pinch of salt

1 To make the pie dough, place the flour and sugar in a large bowl and rub in the butter. Add the cold water and work the mixture together until a soft pie dough has formed. Wrap and leave to chill for 30 minutes.

2 Roll out the dough and line a 10-inch loose-bottomed quiche pan. Prick the pie dough with a fork and chill for 30 minutes.

3 Line the pie shell with foil and dried beans and bake in a preheated oven at 375°F for 15 minutes. Remove the foil and beans and cook the pie shell for a further 15 minutes.

4 To make the filling, mix the orange rind, orange juice and breadcrumbs in a bowl. Stir in the lemon juice and light cream. Melt the butter and sugar over a low heat. Remove the pan from the heat, add the 2 egg

yolks, the salt, and the breadcrumb mixture and stir to combine.

5 Whisk the egg whites with the salt until they form soft peaks. Fold them into the egg yolk mixture.

6 Pour the filling mixture into the pie shell. Bake in a preheated oven at 325°F for about 45 minutes, or until just set. Cool slightly and serve warm.

Coconut Cream Tart

Serves 6-8

INGREDIENTS

PIE DOUGH:
1¼ cups all-purpose flour
5 tsp superfine sugar
½ cup butter, cut into
    small pieces
1 tbsp water

FILLING:
2 cups milk
4½ ounces creamed coconut
3 egg yolks
½ cup superfine sugar
½ cup all-purpose flour, sifted
⅓ cup shredded coconut

¼ cup chopped candied pineapple
2 tbsp rum or pineapple juice
1¼ cups whipping cream, whipped

1 To make the pie dough, place the flour and sugar in a bowl and rub in the butter. Add the water and work the mixture together until a soft pie dough has formed. Wrap and chill for 30 minutes.

2 On a lightly floured surface, roll out the dough and line a 10-inch loose-bottomed quiche pan. Prick the pie dough with a fork and chill

for 30 minutes. Line the pie shell with foil and dried beans and bake in a preheated oven at 375°F for 15 minutes. Remove the foil and beans and cook the pie shell for a further 15 minutes. Let cool.

3 To make the filling, bring the milk and creamed coconut to just below boiling point in a pan, stirring to melt the coconut.

4 Whisk the egg yolks with the sugar until fluffy. Whisk in the flour. Add the hot milk, stirring. Return the mixture to the pan and gently heat for 8 minutes, until thick, stirring. Let cool.

5 Stir in the coconut, pineapple, rum, or pineapple juice, and spread the filling in the pie shell. Cover with the whipped cream and chill.

Pine Nut Tart

Serves 8

INGREDIENTS

PIE DOUGH:

1 ¼ cups all-purpose flour

5 tsp superfine sugar

½ cup butter, cut into
   small pieces

1 tbsp water

FILLING:

1¼ cups cottage cheese

4 tbsp heavy cream

3 eggs

½ cup superfine sugar

grated rind of 1 orange

1 cup pine nuts

1 To make the pie dough, place the flour and sugar in a bowl and rub in the butter with your fingertips. Add the water and work the mixture together until a soft pie dough has formed. Wrap and chill for 30 minutes.

2 On a lightly floured surface, roll out the dough and line a 10-inch loose-bottomed quiche pan. Prick the pie dough all over with a fork and chill for 30 minutes.

3 Line the pie shell with foil and dried beans and bake in a preheated oven at 375°F for 15 minutes. Remove the foil and beans and cook the pie shell for a further 15 minutes.

4 To make the filling, beat together the curd cheese, cream, eggs, sugar, orange rind, and half of the pine nuts. Pour the filling into the prepared pie shell and sprinkle with the remaining pine nuts.

5 Bake in the oven at 325°F for 35 minutes, or until just set. Set aside and cool slightly before serving.

Candied Peel & Nut Tart

Serves 8

INGREDIENTS

PIE DOUGH:

1¼ cups all-purpose flour

5 tsp superfine sugar

½ cup butter, cut into
    small pieces

1 tbsp water

FILLING:

6 tbsp butter

¼ cup superfine sugar

⅓ cup set honey

¾ cup heavy cream

1 egg, beaten

1¾ cups mixed nuts

⅞ cup candied peel

1 To make the pie dough, place the flour and sugar in a bowl and rub in the pieces of butter with your fingertips. Add the water and work the mixture together to form a soft pie dough. Wrap and chill for 30 minutes.

2 On a lightly floured surface, roll out the dough and line a 10-inch loose-bottomed quiche pan. Prick the pie dough all over with a fork and chill for 30 minutes.

3 Line the pie shell with foil and dried beans and bake in a preheated oven at 375°F for 15 minutes. Remove the foil and beans and cook for 15 minutes longer.

4 To make the filling, melt the butter, sugar, and honey in a pan. Stir in the cream and beaten egg, then add the nuts and candied peel. Cook over a low heat, stirring, for 2 minutes, until the mixture is a pale golden color.

5 Pour the filling into the pie shell and bake for 15–20 minutes, or until just set. Let cool, then serve in slices.

Apricot & Cranberry Frangipane Tart

Serves 8-10

INGREDIENTS

PIE DOUGH:
1 1/4 cups all-purpose flour
1/2 cup superfine sugar
1/2 cup butter, cut into
    small pieces
1 tbsp water

FILLING:
7/8 cup sweet butter
1 cup superfine sugar
1 egg
2 egg yolks
1/3 cup all-purpose flour, sifted

1 1/2 cups ground almonds
4 tbsp heavy cream
14 1/2 ounce can apricot
    halves, drained
1 cup fresh cranberries

1 Place the flour and sugar in a bowl and rub in the butter. Add the water and work the mixture together until a soft pie dough has formed. Wrap and chill for 30 minutes.

2 Roll out the dough and line a 10-inch loose-bottomed quiche pan. Prick the dough with a fork and chill for 30 minutes.

3 Line the pie shell with foil and dried beans and bake in a preheated oven at 375°F for 15 minutes. Remove the foil and beans, return the pie shell to the oven and cook for a further 10 minutes.

4 To make the filling, cream together the butter and sugar until light and fluffy. Beat in the egg and egg yolks,

then stir in the flour, almonds, and cream.

5 Place the apricot halves and cranberries on the bottom of the pie shell and spoon the filling over the top.

6 Bake in the oven for about 1 hour, or until the topping is just set. Cool slightly, then serve warm or cold.

White Chocolate & Almond Tart

Serves 8

INGREDIENTS

PIE DOUGH:
1 ¼ cups all-purpose flour
5 tsp superfine sugar
½ cup butter, cut into
    small pieces
1 tbsp water

FILLING:
¾ cup light corn syrup
2 tbsp butter
⅓ cup light brown sugar
3 eggs, lightly beaten
½ cup whole blanched almonds,
    roughly chopped

3½ ounces white chocolate,
    roughly chopped
cream, to serve (optional)

1 To make the pie shell, place the flour and sugar in a mixing bowl and rub in the butter with your fingers. Add the water and work the mixture together until a soft pie dough has formed. Wrap and chill for 30 minutes.

2 On a lightly floured surface, roll out the dough and line a 10-inch loose-bottomed quiche pan. Prick the pie dough all over with a fork and chill for 30 minutes. Line the pie shell with foil and dried beans and bake in a preheated oven at 375°F for 15 minutes. Remove the foil and beans, return the pie shell to the oven and cook for a further 15 minutes.

3 To make the filling, gently melt the syrup, butter, and sugar together in a saucepan. Remove from the heat and let cool slightly. Add the beaten eggs, almonds, and chocolate, and stir until well blended.

4 Pour the chocolate and nut filling into the prepared pie shell and cook in the oven for 30–35 minutes, or until just set. Let cool before removing from the pan. Serve with cream, if desired.

Mincemeat & Grape Jalousie

Serves 4

INGREDIENTS

1 pound 2 ounces fresh ready-made puff pastry	3½ ounces grapes, seeded and halved	raw crystal sugar, for sprinkling
14½ ounce jar mincemeat	1 egg, for glazing	

1 Lightly grease a cookie sheet with a little butter.

2 On a lightly floured surface, roll out the dough and cut it into 2 rectangles.

3 Place one dough rectangle onto the prepared cookie sheet and brush the edges with water.

4 Combine the mincemeat and grapes in a mixing bowl. Spread the mixture over the dough rectangle on the cookie sheet, leaving a 1-inch border all around.

5 Fold the second dough rectangle in half lengthwise. Using a sharp knife, carefully cut a series of parallel lines across the folded edge, leaving a 1-inch border.

6 Open out the puff pastry dough rectangle and lay it over the mincemeat. Seal down the edges of the dough and press together well.

7 Flute and crimp the edges of the dough. Lightly brush the dough with the beaten egg and sprinkle with a little raw crystal sugar.

8 Bake the jalousie in a preheated oven at 425°F for about 15 minutes. Lower the heat to 350°F and cook for a further 30 minutes, until the jalousie is well risen and golden brown. Cool on a wire rack before serving.

COOK'S TIP

For an enhanced festive flavor, stir 2 tbsp sherry into the mincemeat.

Pear Tarts

Makes 6

INGREDIENTS

9 ounces fresh ready-made
    puff pastry
8 tsp light brown sugar

2 tbsp butter (plus extra
    for brushing)
1 tbsp finely chopped
    preserved ginger

3 pears, peeled, halved, and cored
cream, to serve

1 On a lightly floured
    surface, roll out the
dough. Cut out six rounds
4 inches in diameter

2 Place the rounds on
    a large cookie sheet
and chill in the refrigerator
for 30 minutes.

3 Cream together
    the brown sugar and
butter in a small bowl,
then stir in the chopped
preserved ginger.

4 Prick the pastry rounds
    all over with a fork and
spread a little of the ginger
mixture onto each one.

5 Slice the pears halves
    lengthwise, keeping
the pears intact at the tip.
Carefully fan out the
slices slightly.

6 Place a fanned-out pear
    half on top of each
dough round. Make small
flutes around the edge of
the dough rounds and
generously brush each pear
half with melted butter.

7 Bake in a preheated
    oven at 400°F for
15–20 minutes, until
the pastry is well risen
and golden in color. Serve
warm with a little cream.

COOK'S TIP

*If you prefer, serve these tarts
with vanilla ice cream for a
delicious dessert.*

Crème Brûlée Tarts

Makes 6

INGREDIENTS

PIE DOUGH:
1¼ cups all-purpose flour
5 tsp superfine sugar
½ cup butter, cut into
    small pieces.
1 tbsp water

FILLING:
4 egg yolks
¼ cup superfine sugar
1¾ cups heavy cream
1 tsp vanilla extract
raw crystal sugar,
    for sprinkling

1 Place the flour and sugar in a large mixing bowl and rub in the butter. Add the water and work the mixture together until a soft pie dough has formed. Wrap and chill for 30 minutes.

2 Roll out the dough to line six 4-inch tart pans. Prick the bottom of the pie dough all over with a fork and chill in the refrigerator for 20 minutes.

3 Line the pie shells with foil and dried beans and bake in a preheated oven at 375°F for 15 minutes. Remove the foil and beans and cook the pie shells for a further 10 minutes, until crisp and golden. Let cool.

4 Meanwhile, make the filling. In a bowl, beat the egg yolks and sugar until pale. Heat the cream and vanilla extract in a pan until just below boiling point, then pour it onto the egg mixture, whisking constantly.

5 Place the mixture in a pan and bring to just below a boil, stirring, until thick. Do not allow to boil or it will curdle.

6 Let the mixture cool slightly, then pour it into the tart pans. Cool and then chill overnight.

7 Sprinkle the tarts with the sugar. Place under a preheated broiler for a few minutes. Cool, then chill for 2 hours before serving.

Mini Frangipane Tartlets with Lime

Makes 12

INGREDIENTS

1 cup all-purpose flour
¹⁄₃ cup butter, softened
1 tsp grated lime rind
1 tbsp lime juice
4 tbsp superfine sugar
1 egg

¹⁄₄ cup ground almonds
¹⁄₃ cup confectioners' sugar, sifted
¹⁄₂ tbsp water

1 Reserve 5 teaspoons of the flour and 1 tablespoon of the butter and set aside until required.

2 Rub the remaining butter into the remaining flour, until the mixture resembles fine breadcrumbs. Stir in the lime rind, followed by the lime juice and bring the mixture together to form a soft dough.

3 On a lightly floured surface, roll out the dough thinly. Stamp out twelve 3-inch rounds and line a muffin pan.

4 In a bowl, cream together the reserved butter with the superfine sugar.

5 Mix in the egg, then the ground almonds and the reserved flour.

6 Divide the mixture between the pie shells.

7 Bake in a preheated oven at 400°F for 15 minutes, until set and lightly golden. Remove the tartlets from the pan and let cool.

8 Mix the confectioners' sugar with the water. Drizzle a little of the frosting over each tartlet and serve.

Baked Bean Curd Cheesecake

Serves 6

INGREDIENTS

2¹/₂ cups crushed graham crackers
4 tbsp vegan margarine, melted
¹/₄ cups pitted, chopped dates
4 tbsp lemon juice

rind of 1 lemon
3 tbsp water
12 ounces firm bean curd
²/₃ cup apple juice

1 banana, mashed
1 tsp vanilla extract
1 mango, peeled and chopped

1 Lightly grease a 7-inch round loose-bottomed cake pan with a little butter.

2 Mix together the graham cracker crumbs and melted margarine in a bowl. Press the mixture into the base of the prepared pan.

3 Put the chopped dates, lemon juice, lemon rind, and water into a saucepan and bring to a boil. Simmer for 5 minutes until the dates are soft, then mash them roughly with a fork.

4 Place the mixture in a blender or food processor with the bean curd, apple juice, mashed banana, and vanilla extract and process until the mixture is a thick, smooth purée.

5 Pour the bean curd purée into the prepared graham cracker crumb base.

6 Bake in a preheated oven at 350°F for 30–40 minutes, until lightly golden in color. Cool in the pan, then chill thoroughly before serving.

7 Place the chopped mango in a blender and process until smooth. Serve it as a sauce with the chilled cheesecake.

Pineapple Upside-Down Cake

Serves 6

INGREDIENTS

15 ounce can unsweetened
   pineapple pieces, drained and
   juice reserved

4 tsp cornstarch

3 tbsp light brown sugar

4 tbsp vegan margarine, cut into
   small pieces

¹/₂ cup water

rind of 1 lemon

SPONGE:

¹/₄ cup sunflower oil

¹/₃ cup light brown sugar

²/₃ cup water

1¹/₄ cups all-purpose flour

2 tsp baking powder

1 tsp ground cinnamon

1 Grease a deep 7-inch cake pan. Mix the reserved juice from the pineapple with the cornstarch until it forms a smooth paste. Put the paste in a saucepan with the sugar, vegan margarine, and water and stir over a low heat until the sugar has dissolved. Bring to a boil and simmer for 2–3 minutes, until thickened. Cool the mixture slightly.

2 To make the sponge, place the oil, sugar, and water in a saucepan. Heat gently until the sugar has dissolved; do not allow it to boil. Remove from the heat and cool. Sift the flour, baking powder, and ground cinnamon into a mixing bowl. Add the cooled sugar syrup and beat well to form a batter.

3 Place the pineapple pieces and lemon rind on the bottom of the pan and pour 4 tbsp of the pineapple syrup over the pineapple. Spoon the sponge batter on top.

4 Bake in a preheated oven at 350°F for 35–40 minutes, until set and a knife inserted into the center comes out clean. Invert onto a plate, let stand for 5 minutes, then remove the pan. Serve the cake with the remaining syrup.

Date & Apricot Tart

Serves 6-8

INGREDIENTS

1¾ cups plain whole-wheat flour	tbsp water	1 tsp ground cinnamon
½ cup ground mixed nuts	2 cups dried apricots, chopped	grated rind of 1 lemon
⅓ cup vegan margarine, cut into small pieces	1⅓ cups pitted, chopped dates	soy custard, to serve (optional)
	2 cups apple juice	

1 Place the flour and ground nuts in a mixing bowl and rub in the margarine with your fingertips until the mixture resembles breadcrumbs. Stir in the water and bring together to form a dough. Wrap the dough and chill for 30 minutes.

2 Meanwhile, place the apricots and dates in a saucepan with the apple juice, cinnamon, and lemon rind. Bring to a boil, cover, and simmer for 15 minutes, until the fruit softens and can be mashed to a purée.

3 Reserve a small ball of pie dough for making lattice strips. On a lightly floured surface, roll out the rest of the dough to form a round and use to line a 9-inch loose-bottomed quiche pan.

4 Spread the fruit filling over the base of the pie dough. Roll out the reserved pie dough and cut into strips ½ inch wide. Cut the strips to fit the tart and twist them across the top of the fruit to form a lattice pattern. Moisten the edges of the strips with water and seal to the rim.

5 Bake in a preheated oven at 400°F for 25–30 minutes, until golden brown. Cut into slices and serve with soy custard, if using.

Fruit Crumble

Serves 6

INGREDIENTS

6 eating pears, peeled, cored,
    quartered, and sliced
1 tbsp chopped preserved ginger
1 tbsp molasses
2 tbsp orange juice

TOPPING:
1½ cups all-purpose flour
⅓ cup vegan margarine, cut into
    small pieces
¼ cup slivered almonds

⅓ cup dried oats
⅛ cup molasses
soy custard, to serve

1 Lightly grease a 5 cup
ovenproof dish.

2 In a bowl, mix together
the pears, ginger,
molasses, and orange juice.
Spoon the mixture into
the prepared dish.

3 To make the crumble
topping, sift the flour
into a mixing bowl and rub
in the margarine with your
fingers until well combined
and the mixture resembles
fine breadcrumbs. Stir in
the slivered almonds, oats,
and molasses. Mix together
until all the ingredients
are well combined.

4 Sprinkle the crumble
topping evenly over
the pear and ginger
mixture in the dish, to
cover the fruit completely.

5 Bake the crumble
in a preheated oven
at 375°F for 30 minutes,
until the topping is golden
and the fruit is tender.
Serve with soy custard,
if using.

VARIATION

*Stir 1 tsp apple
pie spice into the
crumble mixture in
step 3 for added flavor,
if you prefer.*

Lemon Mascarpone Cheesecake

Serves 8

INGREDIENTS

1½ tbsp unsalted butter
2 cups crushed ginger snaps
2 tbsp preserved ginger

2¼ cups mascarpone cheese
finely grated rind and juice of
  2 lemons

1 cup superfine sugar
2 large eggs, separated
fruit coulis (see Cook's Tip), to serve

1 Grease and line the base of a 10-inch springform cake pan or loose-bottomed pan.

2 Melt the butter in a pan and stir in the crushed cookies and chopped ginger. Use the mixture to line the pan, pressing the mixture about ½ inch up the sides.

3 Beat together the cheese, lemon rind and juice, sugar, and egg yolks until smooth.

4 Whisk the egg whites until they are stiff and fold into the cheese and lemon mixture, blending well.

5 Pour the mixture into the cookie shell in the pan and bake in a preheated oven at 350°F for 35–45 minutes, until just set. Don't worry if it cracks or sinks– this is quite normal.

6 Leave the cheesecake in the pan to cool. Serve with fruit coulis (see Cook's Tip).

COOK'S TIP

Fruit coulis can be made by cooking 14 ounces fruit, such as blueberries, for 5 minutes with 2 tablespoons of water. Strain the mixture, then stir in 1 tablespoon (or more to taste) of sifted confectioner's sugar. Cool before serving.

VARIATION

Ricotta cheese can be used instead of the mascarpone to make an equally delicious cheesecake. It should be rubbed through a strainer before use to remove any lumps.

Breads & Savories

Freshly baked bread has never been easier to make, especially with the easy-blend yeasts available nowadays. In this chapter, ⅕ ounce sachets of easy-blend dried yeast have been used as it is easy to obtain, simple to use, and gives good results. If you want to use fresh yeast, replace one sachet of easy-blend yeast with 1 ounce of fresh yeast. Blend the fresh yeast into the warm liquid and add 1 teaspoon of sugar. Add to the flour and continue as usual.

Always choose a strong white or brown flour for the bread recipes using yeast, it contains a high proportion of gluten, the protein which gives the dough its elasticity. Always knead the dough thoroughly—this can be done in an electric mixer with the dough hook attachment for about 5–8 minutes, but kneading by hand is most enjoyable, and allows the cook the pleasure of relieving their aggression, and stress upon the dough!

This chapter also includes a selection of savories, including a tasty selection of pies, pastries, and flans to create a whole medley of delicious dishes that can be used as part of a main meal.

Teacakes

Serves 12

INGREDIENTS

4 cups strong white
bread flour
1 packet active dry yeast

3 tbsp superfine sugar
1 tsp salt
2 tbsp butter, cut into
small pieces

1¼ cups lukewarm milk
½ cup luxury dried fruit mix
honey, for brushing

1 Thoroughly grease several cookie sheets.

2 Sift the flour into a large mixing bowl. Stir in the yeast, sugar, and salt. Rub in the butter with your fingers until the mixture resembles fine breadcrumbs. Add the milk and mix all of the ingredients together to form a soft dough.

3 Place the dough on a lightly floured surface and knead for about 5 minutes (alternatively, you can knead the dough with an electric mixer with a dough hook).

4 Place the dough in a greased bowl, cover, and let rise in a warm place for 1–1½ hours, until it has doubled in size.

5 Knead the dough again for a few minutes and knead in the fruit. Divide the dough into 12 rounds and place on the cookie sheets. Cover and leave for 1 hour longer, or until springy to the touch when pressed lightly with a finger.

6 Bake in a preheated oven at 400°F for 20 minutes. Brush the teacakes with honey while still warm.

7 Cool the teacakes on a wire rack before serving them split in half. Spread with butter and serve.

Cinnamon Swirls

Makes 12

INGREDIENTS

2 cups strong white
    bread flour
1/2 tsp salt
1 packet active dry yeast

2 tbsp butter, cut into
    small pieces
1 egg, beaten
1/2 cup warm milk
2 tbsp maple syrup

FILLING:
4 tbsp butter, softened
3 tbsp light brown sugar
2 tsp ground cinnamon
1/3 cup currants

1 Thoroughly grease a 9-inch square baking pan.

2 Sift the flour and salt into a mixing bowl. Stir in the yeast. Rub in the butter with your fingertips until the mixture resembles breadcrumbs. Add the egg and milk and mix everything to form a dough.

3 Place the dough in a greased bowl, cover, and leave in a warm place for about 40 minutes, or until doubled in size.

4 Knead the dough lightly for 1 minute to punch down, then roll out to a rectangle 12 × 9 inches.

5 To make the filling, cream together the butter, brown sugar, and cinnamon, until light and fluffy. Spread the filling over the dough, leaving a 1-inch border. Sprinkle the currants on top.

6 Roll up the dough like a jelly roll, from a long edge, and press to seal. Cut the roll into 12 slices. Place them in the pan, cover, and leave for 30 minutes.

7 Bake in a preheated oven at 375°F for 20–30 minutes, or until well risen. Brush with the syrup and cool slightly before serving.

Cinnamon & Currant Loaf

Makes a 2-pound loaf

INGREDIENTS

3 cups all-purpose flour
pinch of salt
1 tbsp baking powder
1 tbsp ground cinnamon

²/₃ cup butter, cut
  into small pieces
³/₄ cup light brown sugar
³/₄ cup currants

finely grated rind of 1 orange
5–6 tbsp orange juice
6 tbsp milk
2 eggs, lightly beaten

1 Thoroughly grease a 2-pound loaf pan and line the base with baking parchment.

2 Sift the flour, salt, baking powder, and ground cinnamon into a bowl. Rub in the butter pieces with your fingertips until the mixture resembles coarse breadcrumbs.

3 Stir in the sugar, currants, and orange rind. Beat the orange juice, milk, and eggs together and add to the dry ingredients. Mix well.

4 Spoon the mixture into the prepared pan. Make a slight dip in the middle of the mixture to help it rise evenly.

5 Bake in a preheated oven at 350°F for about 1–1 hour 10 minutes, or until a toothpick inserted into the center of the loaf comes out clean.

6 Let the loaf cool before turning out of the pan. Transfer to a wire rack and cool completely before slicing and serving.

COOK'S TIP

Once you have added the liquid to the dry ingredients, work as quickly as possible because the baking powder is activated by the liquid.

Orange, Banana, & Cranberry Loaf

Serves 8–10

INGREDIENTS

1¹/₂ cups self-rising flour
¹/₂ tsp baking powder
1 cup light brown sugar
2 bananas, mashed

¹/₄ cup chopped candied peel
¹/₄ cup chopped mixed nuts
¹/₂ cup dried cranberries
5–6 tbsp orange juice

2 eggs, beaten
²/₃ cup sunflower oil
¹/₃ cup confectioners' sugar, sifted
grated rind of 1 orange

1 Thotoughly grease a 2-pound loaf pan and line the base with baking parchment.

2 Sift the flour and baking powder into a large mixing bowl. Stir in the sugar, bananas, chopped candied peel, chopped nuts, and cranberries.

3 Stir the orange juice, eggs, and oil together until well combined. Add the mixture to the dry ingredients and mix until well blended. Pour the mixture into the prepared loaf pan.

4 Bake in a preheated oven at 350°F for about 1 hour, until firm to the touch or until a toothpick inserted into the center of the loaf comes out clean.

5 Turn out the loaf and cool on a wire rack.

6 Mix the confectioners' sugar with a little water and drizzle the frosting over the loaf. Sprinkle the orange rind over the top. Let the frosting set before serving the loaf in slices.

COOK'S TIP

This tea bread will keep for a couple of days. Wrap it carefully and store in a cool, dry place.

Banana & Date Loaf

Serves 6-8

INGREDIENTS

2 cups self-rising flour

¹/₃ cup butter, cut into
    small pieces

¹/₃ cup superfine sugar

⁷/₈ cup chopped, pitted dates

2 bananas, roughly mashed

2 eggs, lightly beaten

2 tbsp clear honey

1 Thoroughly grease
a 2-pound loaf pan and
line the base with baking
parchment.

2 Sift the flour into
a large mixing bowl.

3 Rub the butter
into the flour with your
fingertips until the mixture
resembles fine breadcrumbs.

4 Stir the sugar,
chopped dates,
bananas, beaten eggs,
and honey into the dry
ingredients. Mix together
to form a soft dropping
consistency.

5 Spoon the mixture
into the prepared loaf
pan and level the surface
with the back of a knife.

6 Bake in a preheated
oven at 325°F for about
1 hour, or until golden
and a toothpick inserted into
the center comes out clean.

7 Let the loaf cool in
the pan before turning
out and transferring to
a wire rack.

8 Serve the loaf
warm or cold, cut
into thick slices.

COOK'S TIP

*This tea bread will keep for
several days if stored in an
airtight container and kept
in a cool, dry place.*

Crown Loaf

Makes one loaf

INGREDIENTS

2 cups strong white bread flour
$\frac{1}{2}$ tsp salt
1 packet active dry yeast
2 tbsp butter, cut into
  small pieces
$\frac{1}{2}$ cup lukewarm milk
1 egg, beaten

FILLING:
4 tbsp butter, softened
3 tbsp light brown sugar
$\frac{1}{4}$ cup chopped hazelnuts
2 tbsp chopped preserved ginger
$\frac{1}{4}$ cup candied peel
1 tbsp rum or brandy

$\frac{2}{3}$ cup confectioners' sugar
2 tbsp lemon juice

1 Grease a cookie sheet. Sift the flour and salt into a bowl. Stir in the yeast. Rub in the butter. Add the milk and egg and mix together to form a dough.

2 Place the dough in a greased bowl, cover, and leave in a warm place for 40 minutes, until doubled in size. Knead the dough lightly for 1 minute to punch down. Roll out to a rectangle 12 × 9 inches.

3 Cream together the butter and sugar until light and fluffy. Stir in the hazelnuts, ginger, candied peel, and rum. Spread the filling over the dough, leaving a 1-inch border.

4 Roll up the dough from the long edge, to form a sausage shape. Cut into 2-inch slices and place on the cookie sheet in a circle with the slices just touching. Cover and let

the dough rise in a warm place for 30 minutes.

5 Bake in a preheated oven at 325°F for 20–30 minutes, or until golden. Meanwhile, mix the confectioners' sugar with enough lemon juice to form a thin frosting.

6 Let the loaf cool slightly before drizzling the whole circle with frosting.

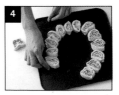

Date & Honey Loaf

Makes one loaf

INGREDIENTS

1 ¼ cups strong white bread flour
¼ cup strong brown bread flour
½ tsp salt

1 packet active dry yeast
¾ cup lukewarm water
3 tbsp sunflower oil

3 tbsp honey
1 ½ cup chopped, pitted dates
2 tbsp sesame seeds

1 Grease a 2-pound loaf pan. Sift the white and brown flours into a large mixing bowl, stir in the salt and yeast.

2 Pour in the water, oil, and honey. Mix everything together to form a dough.

3 Place the dough on a lightly floured surface and knead for about 5 minutes, until smooth.

4 Place the dough in a greased bowl, cover, and let rise in a warm place for about 1 hour, or until doubled in size.

5 Knead in the dates and sesame seeds. Shape the dough and place in the pan.

6 Cover and leave in a warm place for another 30 minutes, or until springy to the touch.

7 Bake in a preheated oven at 425°F for 30 minutes, or until a hollow sound can be heard when the base of the loaf is tapped with the knuckles.

8 Transfer the loaf to a wire rack and let it cool. Serve the loaf, cut into thick slices.

VARIATION

Replace the sesame seeds with sunflower seeds for a slightly different texture, if you prefer.

COOK'S TIP

If you cannot find a warm place, sit the bowl over a saucepan of warm water.

Pumpkin Loaf

Serves 6-8

INGREDIENTS

3¹/₂ cups chopped pumpkin flesh
¹/₂ cup butter, softened
³/₄ cup superfine sugar

2 eggs, beaten
2 cups all-purpose flour, sifted
1¹/₂ tsp baking powder

¹/₂ tsp salt
1 tsp ground apple pie spice
¹/₃ cup pumpkin seeds

1 Grease a 2-pound loaf pan with oil.

2 Wrap the pumpkin pieces in buttered foil. Cook in a preheated oven at 400°F for about 30–40 minutes, until they are cooked through and tender.

3 Let the pumpkin cool completely before mashing well to make a thick purée.

4 In a bowl, cream the butter and sugar together until light and fluffy. Add the eggs, a little at a time.

5 Stir in the pumpkin purée. Fold in the flour, baking powder, salt, and apple pie spice.

6 Fold the pumpkin seeds through the mixture. Spoon the mixture into the prepared loaf pan.

7 Bake in a preheated oven at 325°F for about 1¹/₄–1¹/₂ hours, or until a toothpick inserted into the center of the loaf comes out clean.

8 Let the loaf cool and serve buttered, if desired.

COOK'S TIP

To ensure that the pumpkin purée is dry, place it in a saucepan over a medium heat for a few minutes, stirring frequently, until it is thick.

Tropical Fruit Bread

Makes one loaf

INGREDIENTS

3 cups strong white bread flour
5 tbsp bran
$\frac{1}{2}$ tsp salt
$\frac{1}{2}$ tsp ground ginger
1 packet active dry yeast
2 tbsp light brown sugar

2 tbsp butter, cut into
    small pieces
generous 1 cup lukewarm water
$\frac{1}{2}$ cup finely chopped,
    candied pineapple

3 tbsp finely chopped dried mango
$\frac{2}{3}$ cup shredded coconut, toasted
1 egg, beaten
2 tbsp coconut shreds

1 Thoroughly grease a cookie sheet. Sift the flour into a large mixing bowl. Stir in the bran, salt, ginger, yeast, and sugar. Rub in the butter with your fingers, then add the water, and mix to form a dough.

2 On a lightly floured surface, knead the dough for about 5–8 minutes, or until smooth (alternatively, use an electric mixer with a dough hook).

Place the dough in a greased bowl, cover, and let rise in a warm place until doubled in size.

3 Knead the candied pineapple, dried mango, and shredded coconut into the dough. Shape into a round loaf and place on the cookie sheet. Score the top with the back of a knife. Cover and leave for a further 30 minutes in a warm place.

4 Brush the loaf with the egg and sprinkle with the 2 tbsp coconut. Bake in a preheated oven at 425°F for 30 minutes, or until golden in color.

5 Let the bread cool on a wire rack before serving.

Citrus Bread

Makes one loaf

INGREDIENTS

4 cups strong white bread flour	5–6 tbsp orange juice	1 orange
1/2 tsp salt	4 tbsp lemon juice	1 lemon
1/4 cup superfine sugar	3–4 tbsp lime juice	1 lime
1 packet active dry yeast	2/3 cup lukewarm water	2 tbsp clear honey
4 tbsp butter, cut into small pieces		

1 Lightly grease a cookie sheet.

2 Sift the flour and salt into a mixing bowl. Stir in the sugar and yeast.

3 Rub the butter into the mixture using your fingers. Add all of the fruit juices and the water and mix to form a dough.

4 Place the dough on a lightly floured counter and knead for 5 minutes (alternatively, use an electric mixer with a dough hook). Place the dough in a greased bowl, cover, and let rise in a warm place for 1 hour.

5 Meanwhile, grate the rind of the orange, lemon, and lime. Knead the fruit rinds into the dough.

6 Divide the dough into 2 balls, one slightly bigger than the other.

7 Place the larger ball on the cookie sheet and place the smaller one on top.

8 Push a floured finger through the center of the dough. Cover and let rise for about 40 minutes or until springy to the touch.

9 Bake in a preheated oven at 425°F for 35 minutes. Remove from the oven and glaze with the honey.

410

Mango Twist Bread

Makes one loaf

INGREDIENTS

4 cups strong white bread flour
1 tsp salt
1 packet active dry yeast
1 tsp ground ginger
3 tbsp light brown sugar

3 tbsp butter, cut into small pieces
1 small mango, peeled, cored,
    and puréed
generous 1 cup lukewarm water
2 tbsp clear honey

²/₃ cup golden raisins
1 egg, beaten
confectioners' sugar,
    for dusting

1 Thoroughly grease a cookie sheet. Sift the flour and salt into a large mixing bowl and stir in the yeast, ground ginger, and brown sugar. Rub in the butter with your fingers.

2 Stir in the mango purée, water, and honey and mix together to form a dough.

3 Place the dough on a lightly floured surface and knead for about 5 minutes, until smooth (alternatively, use an electric mixer with a dough hook). Place the dough in a greased bowl, cover, and let rise in a warm place for about 1 hour, until it has doubled in size.

4 Knead in the golden raisins and shape the dough into 2 sausage shapes, each 10 inches long. Carefully twist the 2 pieces together and pinch the ends to seal. Place the dough on the cookie sheet, cover and let rise in a warm place for another 40 minutes.

5 Brush the loaf with the egg and bake in a preheated oven, at 425°F for 30 minutes, or until golden brown. Leave on a wire rack to cool completely. Dust with confectioners' sugar before serving.

Chocolate Bread

Makes one loaf

INGREDIENTS

4 cups strong white bread flour
1/4 cup unsweetened cocoa
1 tsp salt
1 packet active dry yeast

2 tbsp light brown sugar
1 tbsp oil
1 1/2 cups lukewarm water

1 Lightly grease a 2-pound loaf pan.

2 Sift the flour and the unsweetened cocoa into a large mixing bowl.

3 Stir in the salt, yeast, and brown sugar.

4 Pour in the oil along with the water and mix the ingredients together to make a dough.

5 Place the dough on a lightly floured surface and knead for about 5 minutes.

6 Place the dough in a greased bowl, cover, and let rise in a warm place for 1 hour, or until the dough has doubled in size.

7 Punch down the dough and shape it into a loaf. Place the dough into the prepared pan, cover, and then let rise in a warm place for a further 30 minutes.

8 Bake the dough in a preheated oven at 400°F for 25–30 minutes, or until a hollow sound can be heard when the base of the bread is tapped.

9 Transfer the chocolate bread to a wire rack and cool. Cut into slices to serve.

COOK'S TIP

This bread can be sliced and spread with butter or it can be lightly toasted.

Soda Bread

Makes one loaf

INGREDIENTS

2½ cups whole-wheat flour

2½ cups all-purpose flour

2 tsp baking powder

1 tsp baking soda

2 tbsp superfine sugar

1 tsp salt

1 egg, beaten

1¾ cups unsweetened yogurt

1 Thoroughly grease and flour a cookie sheet.

2 Sift the flours, baking powder, baking soda, sugar, and salt into a large bowl.

3 In a mixing bowl, beat together the egg and yogurt and pour the mixture into the dry ingredients. Mix everything together to make a soft and sticky dough.

4 On a lightly floured surface, knead the dough for a few minutes until it is smooth, then shape into a round loaf about 2 inches deep.

5 Transfer the dough to the cookie sheet. Mark a cross shape in the center of the top of the dough.

6 Bake in a preheated oven at 375°F for about 40 minutes, or until the bread is golden brown.

7 Transfer the loaf to a wire rack and cool slightly before serving. Cut the soda bread into slices to serve.

VARIATION

For a delicious fruity version of this soda bread, add ¾ cup of raisins to the dry ingredients in step 2.

Spicy Bread

Makes one loaf

INGREDIENTS

2 cups self-rising flour
$^3/_4$ cup all-purpose flour
1 tsp baking powder

$^1/_4$ tsp salt
$^1/_4$ tsp cayenne pepper
2 tsp curry powder
2 tsp poppy seeds

2 tbsp butter, cut into small pieces
$^2/_3$ cup milk
1 egg, beaten

1 Grease a cookie sheet with butter.

2 Sift the self-rising flour and the all-purpose flour into a large mixing bowl, together with the baking powder, salt, cayenne pepper, curry powder, and poppy seeds.

3 Rub in the butter with your fingers until everything is well mixed together.

4 Add the milk and the beaten egg and mix to a soft dough.

5 Turn the dough out onto a lightly floured surface, then knead the dough lightly for a few minutes.

6 Shape the dough into a round loaf and mark it with a cross shape in the center of the top of the dough.

7 Bake in a preheated oven at 375°F for 45 minutes.

8 Transfer the bread to a wire rack and let cool. Serve in chunks or slices.

COOK'S TIP

If the bread looks as though it is browning too much, cover it with a piece of foil for the remainder of the cooking time.

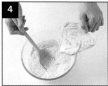

Chili Corn Bread

Makes 12 bars

INGREDIENTS

1 cup all-purpose flour
1 cup cornmeal
1 tbsp baking powder
½ tsp salt

1 green chili, seeded and
    finely chopped
5 scallions, finely chopped
2 eggs

generous ½ cup sour cream
½ cup sunflower oil

1 Grease an 8-inch square cake pan and line the base with baking parchment.

2 In a large bowl, mix the flour, cornmeal, baking powder, and salt together.

3 Add the finely chopped green chili and the scallions to the dry ingredients and mix until well combined.

4 In a large mixing bowl, beat the eggs, together with the sour cream and sunflower oil. Pour the mixture into the bowl of dry

ingredients. Mix all of the ingredients together until well incorporated.

5 Pour the mixture into the prepared cake pan and level the surface with the back of a spoon.

6 Bake in a preheated oven at 400°F for 20–25 minutes, or until the loaf has risen and is lightly browned.

7 Let the bread cool slightly before turning out of the pan. Cut the bread into bars or squares to serve.

VARIATION

Add ¼ cup of corn kernels to the mixture in step 3, if you prefer.

Cheese & Potato Bread

Serves 4

INGREDIENTS

2 cups all-purpose flour	1 cup grated Red Leicester cheese
1 tsp salt	2 cups cooked, mashed potatoes
1/2 tsp mustard powder	3/4 cup water
2 tsp baking powder	1 tbsp oil

1 Lightly grease a cookie sheet.

2 Sift the flour, salt, mustard powder, and baking powder into a mixing bowl.

3 Reserve 2 tbsp of the grated cheese and stir the rest into the bowl with the mashed potatoes. Mix until well combined.

4 Pour in the water and the oil, and stir all the ingredients together (the mixture will be wet at this stage). Mix them all to make a soft dough.

5 Turn out the dough onto a floured surface and shape it into an 8-inch round loaf.

6 Place the loaf on the cookie sheet and mark it into 4 portions with a knife, without cutting through. Sprinkle with the reserved cheese.

7 Bake the loaf in a preheated oven at 425°F for approximately 25–30 minutes.

8 Transfer the bread to a wire rack and let cool. This bread should be served as fresh as possible.

COOK'S TIP

You can use instant potato mix for this bread, if you prefer.

VARIATION

Add 1/3 cup chopped ham to the mixture in step 3, if you prefer.

Cheese & Ham Loaf

Serves 6

INGREDIENTS

2 cups self-rising flour

1 tsp salt

2 tsp baking powder

1 tsp paprika

1/3 cup butter, cut into
    small pieces

1 cup grated sharp cheese

1/2 cup smoked ham, chopped

2 eggs, beaten

2/3 cup milk

1 Thoroughly grease a 1-pound loaf pan and line the base with baking parchment.

2 Sift the flour, salt, baking powder, and paprika into a mixing bowl.

3 Rub in the butter with your fingers until the mixture resembles fine breadcrumbs. Stir in the cheese and ham.

4 Add the beaten eggs and milk to the dry ingredients and mix well.

5 Spoon the cheese and ham mixture into the prepared loaf pan.

6 Bake the mixture in a preheated oven at 350°F for about 1 hour, or until the loaf is well risen.

7 Let the bread cool in the pan, then turn out, and transfer to a wire rack to cool completely.

8 Serve the bread cut into thick slices.

COOK'S TIP

This tasty bread is best eaten on the day it is made, as it does not keep well for very long.

VARIATION

Any grated hard cheese can be used for this bread; use a milder one, if preferred.

Cheese & Chive Bread

Serves 8

INGREDIENTS

2 cups self-rising flour

1 tsp salt

1 tsp mustard powder

1 cup grated sharp cheese

2 tbsp chopped fresh chives

1 egg, beaten

2 tbsp butter, melted

2/3 cup milk

1 Grease a 9-inch square cake pan and line the base with baking parchment.

2 Sift the flour, salt, and mustard powder into a large mixing bowl.

3 Reserve 3 tbsp of the grated sharp cheese for sprinkling over the top of the loaf before baking in the oven.

4 Stir the remaining cheese into the bowl, together with the chopped fresh chives until well combined.

5 Add the beaten egg, melted butter, and milk and blend thoroughly.

6 Pour the mixture into the prepared pan and spread with a knife. Sprinkle with the reserved grated cheese.

7 Bake in a preheated oven at 375°F for about 30 minutes.

8 Let the bread cool slightly in the pan. Turn out the bread onto a wire rack to cool further before serving. Cut into triangles to serve.

COOK'S TIP

You can use any hard sharp cheese of your choice for this recipe.

Garlic Bread Rolls

Makes 8

INGREDIENTS

12 cloves garlic, peeled
1½ cups milk
4 cups strong white
   bread flour

1 tsp salt
1 packet active dry yeast
1 tbsp dried mixed herbs
2 tbsp sunflower oil

1 egg, beaten
milk, for brushing
rock salt, for sprinkling

1 Grease a cookie sheet. Place the garlic cloves and milk in a saucepan, bring to a boil, and simmer gently for 15 minutes. Cool slightly, then process in a blender or food processor to purée the garlic.

2 Sift the flour and the 1 teaspoon of salt into a large mixing bowl and stir in the yeast and mixed herbs.

3 Add the garlic-flavored milk, sunflower oil, and beaten egg to the dry ingredients and mix everything to a dough.

4 Place the dough on a lightly floured counter and knead lightly for a few minutes until smooth and soft.

5 Place the dough in a greased bowl, cover, and let rise in a warm place for about 1 hour, or until doubled in size.

6 Punch down the dough by kneading it vigorously for 2 minutes. Shape into 8 rolls and place on the prepared cookie sheet. Lightly score the top of each roll with a knife,

cover, and leave for 15 minutes.

7 Brush the rolls with a little milk and sprinkle rock salt over the top.

8 Bake in a preheated oven at 425°F for 15–20 minutes.

9 Transfer the rolls to a wire rack and cool completely before serving.

Mini Focaccia

Makes 4

INGREDIENTS

3 cups strong white flour
$\frac{1}{2}$ tsp salt
1 packet active dry yeast
2 tbsp olive oil

$1\frac{1}{8}$ cups lukewarm water
1 cup pitted green or black
olives, halved

TOPPING:
2 red onions, sliced
2 tbsp olive oil
1 tsp sea salt
1 tbsp thyme leaves

1 Lightly oil several cookie sheets. Sift the flour and salt into a large mixing bowl, then stir in the yeast. Pour in the olive oil and water and mix everything together to form a dough.

2 Turn the dough out onto a lightly floured surface and knead it for 10 minutes.

3 Place the dough in a greased bowl, cover, and leave in a warm place for about 1–1½ hours,

until it has doubled in size. Punch down the dough by kneading it again for 1–2 minutes.

4 Knead half of the olives into the dough. Divide the dough into quarters and then shape the quarters into rounds. Place them on the cookie sheets and push your fingers into the dough to achieve a dimpled effect.

5 To make the topping, sprinkle the red onions and remaining olives over

the rounds. Drizzle the olive oil over the top and sprinkle with the sea salt and thyme. Cover and let the dough rise again for 30 minutes.

6 Bake in a preheated oven at 375°F for 20–25 minutes, or until the focaccia are well cooked and golden. Transfer to a wire rack and cool before serving.

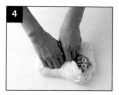

Sun-Dried Tomato Rolls

Makes 8

INGREDIENTS

2 cups strong white
    bread flour
¹/₂ tsp salt
1 packet active dry yeast

¹/₃ cup butter, melted and
    cooled slightly
3 tbsp milk, warmed
2 eggs, beaten

1 cup drained and finely chopped
    sun-dried tomatoes
milk, for brushing

1 Lightly grease a cookie sheet.

2 Sift the flour and salt into a large mixing bowl. Stir in the yeast, then pour in the butter, milk, and eggs. Mix together to form a dough.

3 Turn the dough onto a lightly floured surface and knead for about 5 minutes (alternatively, use an electric mixer with a dough hook).

4 Place the dough in a greased bowl, cover, and let rise in a warm place for 1–1¹/₂ hours, until the dough has doubled in size. Punch down the dough by kneading it lightly for a few minutes.

5 Knead the sun-dried tomatoes into the dough, sprinkling the counter with extra flour as the tomatoes are quite oily.

6 Divide the dough into 8 balls and place them on the prepared cookie sheet. Cover and let rise for about 30 minutes, until the rolls have doubled in size.

7 Lightly brush the rolls with a little milk and bake in a preheated oven, at 450°F for 10–15 minutes, until the rolls are golden brown.

8 Transfer the rolls to a wire rack and cool slightly before serving.

Thyme Crescents

Makes 8

INGREDIENTS

9 ounces fresh ready-made puff
pastry
1/3 cup butter, softened
1 garlic clove, crushed

1 tsp lemon juice
1 tsp dried thyme
salt and pepper

1 Lightly grease a cookie sheet.

2 On a lightly floured surface, roll out the pastry dough to form a 10-inch round and cut into 8 wedges.

3 In a small bowl, mix together the softened butter, garlic clove, lemon juice, and dried thyme until soft. Season to taste.

4 Spread a little of the butter and thyme mixture onto each wedge of pastry dough, dividing it equally between them.

5 Carefully roll up each wedge of pastry dough, starting from the wide end.

6 Arrange the crescents on the prepared cookie sheet and chill for about 30 minutes.

7 Dampen the cookie sheet with cold water. This will create a steamy atmosphere in the oven while the crescents are baking and help the pastries to rise.

8 Bake in a preheated oven at 400°F for 10–15 minutes, until the crescents are well risen and golden.

COOK'S TIP

Dried herbs have a stronger flavor than fresh ones, which makes them perfect for these pastries. The crescents can be made with other dried herbs of your choice, such as rosemary and sage, or mixed herbs.

Cheese & Mustard Scones

Makes 8

INGREDIENTS

2 cups self-rising flour
1 tsp baking powder
pinch of salt
1/3 cup butter, cut into small pieces

1 cup grated sharp cheese
1 tsp mustard powder
2/3 cup milk
pepper

1 Lightly grease a cookie sheet.

2 Sift the flour, baking powder, and salt into a mixing bowl. Rub in the butter with your fingers until the mixture resembles breadcrumbs.

3 Stir in the grated cheese, mustard, and enough milk to form a soft dough.

4 On a lightly floured surface, knead the dough very lightly, then flatten it out with the palm of your hand to a depth of about 1 inch.

5 Cut the dough into 8 wedges with a knife. Brush each one with a little milk and sprinkle with pepper to taste.

6 Bake in a preheated oven at 425°F for 10–15 minutes, until the scones are a golden brown.

7 Transfer the scones to a wire rack and cool slightly before serving.

COOK'S TIP

Scones should be eaten on the day they are made, as they quickly go stale. Serve them split in half and spread with butter.

Cheese Sables

Makes about 35

INGREDIENTS

1 ¼ cups all-purpose flour
1 ½ cup grated sharp cheese

⅔ cup butter, cut into
small pieces

1 egg yolk
sesame seeds, for sprinkling

1 Lightly grease
several cookie sheets.

2 Mix the flour
and cheese together
in a bowl.

3 Add the butter
to the cheese and flour
mixture and mix with your
fingers until combined.

4 Stir in the egg yolk
and mix to form
a dough. Wrap the dough
and chill in the refrigerator
for about 30 minutes.

5 On a lightly floured
surface, roll out
the cheese dough thinly.
Cut out 2½-inch rounds,
re-rolling the trimmings
to make about 35 rounds.

6 Place the rounds
onto the prepared
cookie sheets and sprinkle
the sesame seeds over
the top of them.

7 Bake in a preheated
oven at 400°F for
20 minutes, until the sables
are a light golden color.

8 Transfer the cheese
sables to a wire
rack and cool slightly
before serving.

COOK'S TIP

*Cut out any shape
you like for your savory
biscuits. Children will enjoy
them cut into animal or
other fun shapes.*

Savory Curried Biscuits

Makes 40

INGREDIENTS

³/₄ cup all-purpose flour
1 tsp salt
2 tsp curry powder

1 cup grated mellow hard cheese
1 cup grated Parmesan cheese
¹/₃ cup butter, softened

1 Lightly grease about 4 cookie sheets with butter.

2 Sift the all-purpose flour and salt into a mixing bowl.

3 Add the curry powder, the grated mellow hard cheese, and the grated Parmesan cheese to the mixing bowl and stir until well incorporated. Rub in the softened butter with your fingertips until the mixture comes together to form a soft dough.

4 On a lightly floured surface, roll out the dough thinly to form a rectangle.

5 Using a 2-inch cutter, cut out 40 round biscuits.

6 Arrange the biscuits on the cookie sheets.

7 Bake in a preheated oven at 350°F for 10–15 minutes.

8 Let the biscuits cool slightly on the cookie sheets.

9 Transfer the biscuits to a wire rack until cold and crisp, then serve.

COOK'S TIP

These biscuits can be stored for several days in an airtight metal or plastic container.

Cheese Pudding

Serves 4

INGREDIENTS

2½ cups fresh white breadcrumbs
1 cup grated Swiss cheese
⅔ cup lukewarm milk
½ cup butter, melted

2 eggs, separated
2 tbsp chopped fresh parsley
salt and pepper
salad greens, to serve

1 Thoroughly grease a 5 cup ovenproof dish.

2 Place the breadcrumbs and cheese in a bowl and mix.

3 Pour the milk over the cheese and breadcrumb mixture and stir to mix. Add the melted butter, egg yolks, parsley, and salt and pepper to taste. Mix well.

4 Whisk the egg whites until firm. Fold the cheese mixture into the egg whites.

5 Transfer the mixture to the prepared ovenproof dish.

6 Bake the pudding in a preheated oven at 375°F for about 45 minutes or until golden brown, and slightly risen, and a knife inserted into the middle of the pudding comes out clean.

7 Serve the cheese pudding hot, with salad greens.

VARIATION

Any strongly flavored cheese of your choice can be used instead of the Swiss cheese to make this tasty savory pudding.

COOK'S TIP

For a slightly healthier alternative, make the cheese pudding with fresh whole-wheat breadcrumbs instead of white ones.

Cheese & Onion Pies

Makes 4

INGREDIENTS

3 tbsp vegetable oil
4 onions, peeled and finely sliced
4 garlic cloves, crushed
4 tbsp finely chopped fresh
 parsley
3/4 cup grated sharp cheese
salt and pepper

PIE DOUGH:
1 1/2 cups all-purpose flour
1/2 tsp salt
1/3 cup butter, cut into
 small pieces
3-4 tbsp water

1 Heat the oil in a skillet. Add the onions and garlic and sauté for 10–15 minutes, or until the onions are soft. Remove the pan from the heat and stir in the parsley and cheese, and season.

2 To make the pie dough, sift the flour and salt into a mixing bowl and rub in the butter with your fingertips until the mixture resembles breadcrumbs. Stir in the water and mix to a smooth dough.

3 On a lightly floured surface, roll out the dough and divide it into 8 portions.

4 Roll out each portion to a 4-inch round and use half of the rounds to line 4 individual tart pans.

5 Fill each round with a quarter of the onion mixture. Cover with the remaining 4 pie dough rounds. Make a slit in the top of each pie with the point of a knife

and seal the edges with the back of a teaspoon.

6 Bake in a preheated oven at 425°F for about 20 minutes. The pies can be served hot or cold.

COOK'S TIP

You can prepare the onion filling in advance and store it in the refrigerator.

Red Onion Tart

Serves 4

INGREDIENTS

4 tbsp butter	3 tbsp red wine vinegar	salt and pepper
2 tbsp sugar	2 tbsp fresh thyme leaves	
1 pound 2 ounces red onions, peeled and quartered	8 ounces fresh ready-made puff pastry	

1 Place the butter and sugar in a 9-inch ovenproof skillet and cook over a medium heat until the butter has melted.

2 Add the red onion quarters and sweat them over a low heat for 10–15 minutes, until golden, stirring occasionally.

3 Add the red wine vinegar and fresh thyme leaves to the skillet. Season with salt and pepper to taste, then simmer over a medium heat until the liquid has reduced and the red onion pieces are coated in the buttery sauce.

4 On a lightly floured kitchen counter, roll out the pastry to a round slightly larger than the skillet.

5 Place the dough over the onion mixture and press down, tucking in the edges to seal the pie dough.

6 Bake in a preheated oven at 350°F for about 20–25 minutes. Let the tart stand for 10 minutes.

7 To turn out, place a serving plate over the skillet and carefully invert them both so that the dough crust becomes the base of the tart. Serve the tart warm.

VARIATION

Replace the red onions with shallots, leaving them whole, if you prefer.

Puff Potato Pie

Serves 6

INGREDIENTS

1 pound 9 ounces potatoes, peeled
  and thinly sliced

2 scallions, finely chopped

1 red onion, finely chopped

2/3 cup heavy cream

1 pound 2 ounces fresh ready-
  made puff pastry

2 eggs, beaten

salt and pepper

1 Lightly grease a cookie sheet. Bring a pan of water to a boil, add the sliced potatoes, bring back to a boil, and then simmer for a few minutes. Drain the potato and cool. Dry off any excess moisture with paper towels.

2 In a bowl, mix together the scallions, red onion, and the cooled potato slices. Stir in 2 tablespoons of the cream and plenty of seasoning.

3 Divide the pastry in half and roll out one piece to a 9-inch round. Roll the remaining dough to a 10-inch round.

4 Place the smaller round onto the cookie sheet and top with the potato mixture, leaving a 1-inch border all around. Brush this border with a little of the beaten egg.

5 Top with the larger round of dough, seal well, and crimp the edges of the dough. Cut a steam vent in the middle of the dough and, using the back of a knife, mark with a pattern.

Brush with the beaten egg and bake in a preheated oven at 400°F for 30 minutes.

6 Mix the remaining beaten egg with the rest of the cream and pour into the pie through the steam vent. Return the pie to the oven for 15 minutes. Serve either warm or cold.

Fresh Tomato Tarts

Serves 6

INGREDIENTS

9 ounces fresh ready-made puff
pastry
1 egg, beaten
2 tbsp pesto

6 plum tomatoes, sliced
salt and pepper
fresh thyme leaves, to garnish
(optional)

1 On a lightly floured kitchen counter, roll out the pastry dough to a rectangle measuring 12 × 10 inches.

2 Cut the rectangle in half and divide each half into 3 pieces to make 6 even-size rectangles. Chill in the refrigerator for 20 minutes.

3 Lightly score the edges of the dough rectangles and brush with the beaten egg.

4 Spread the pesto over the rectangles, dividing it equally between them, leaving a 1-inch border on each one.

5 Arrange the tomato slices in a line along the center of each rectangle on top of the pesto.

6 Season well with salt and pepper to taste and lightly sprinkle with fresh thyme leaves, if using.

7 Bake in a preheated oven at 400°F for 15–20 minutes, until well risen and a golden brown color.

8 Transfer the tomato tarts to warm serving plates straight from the oven and serve while they are still piping hot.

VARIATION

Instead of making individual tarts, roll the dough out to form 1 large rectangle. Spoon the pesto on and arrange the tomatoes over the top.

Provençal Tart

Serves 6-8

INGREDIENTS

9 ounces ready-made fresh puff
    pastry
3 tbsp olive oil
2 red bell peppers, seeded and diced

2 green bell peppers, seeded
    and diced
$^2/_3$ cup heavy cream
1 egg

2 zucchini, sliced
salt and pepper

1 Roll out the pastry on a lightly floured surface and line an 8-inch loose-bottomed quiche pan. Chill in the refrigerator for 20 minutes.

2 Meanwhile, heat 2 tbsp of the olive oil in a skillet and sauté the bell peppers for about 8 minutes, until softened, stirring frequently.

3 Whisk the heavy cream and egg together in a large mixing bowl and season to taste with salt and pepper.

Stir in the cooked mixed bell peppers.

4 Heat the remaining oil in a pan and fry the zucchini slices for 4–5 minutes, until they are lightly browned.

5 Carefully pour the egg and bell pepper mixture into the pie shell.

6 Arrange the zucchini slices in a pattern around the edge of the tart.

7 Bake in a preheated oven at 350°F for 35–40 minutes, or until just set and golden brown. Serve hot or cold.

COOK'S TIP

This recipe could be used to make 6 individual tarts—use 6 × 4 inch pans and bake them for 20 minutes.

Celery & Onion Pies

Makes 12

INGREDIENTS

PIE DOUGH:
1 cup all-purpose flour
1/2 tsp salt
2 tbsp butter, cut into
    small pieces
1/4 cup grated sharp cheese
3–4 tbsp water

FILLING:
4 tbsp butter
1 cup finely chopped celery
2 garlic cloves, crushed
1 small onion, finely chopped
1 tbsp all-purpose flour
1/4 cup milk

salt
pinch of cayenne pepper

1 To make the filling, melt the butter, add the celery, garlic, and onion and sauté for 5 minutes, or until softened.

2 Remove from the heat and stir in the flour, then the milk. Heat gently until the mixture is thick, stirring frequently. Season with salt and cayenne pepper. Let cool.

3 To make the pastry, sift together the flour and salt into a mixing bowl and rub in the butter with your fingertips. Stir the cheese into the mixture, together with the cold water, and mix to form a dough.

4 Roll out three-quarters of the dough. Using a 2½-inch cookie cutter, cut out 12 rounds. Line a muffin pan with the rounds.

5 Divide the filling between the pie dough rounds. Roll out the remaining dough and, using a 2-inch cutter, cut out 12 rounds. Place the smaller rounds on top of the pie filling and seal well. Make a slit in each pie and chill for 30 minutes.

6 Bake in a preheated oven at 425°F for 15–20 minutes. Cool in the pan for about 10 minutes before turning out. Serve warm.

Asparagus & Goat's Cheese Tart

Serves 6

INGREDIENTS

9 ounces fresh ready-made
    pie dough
9 ounces asparagus
1 tbsp vegetable oil

1 red onion, finely chopped
1/4 cup chopped hazelnuts
1 3/4 cups ounces goat cheese
2 eggs, beaten

4 tbsp light cream
salt and pepper

1 On a lightly floured surface, roll out the pie dough and line a 10-inch loose-bottomed quiche pan. Prick the base of the pie dough with a fork and chill in the refrigerator for about 30 minutes.

2 Line the pie shell with foil and dried beans and bake blind in a preheated oven at 375°F for approximately 15 minutes.

3 Remove the foil and beans from the pie shell, return the pie shell to the oven and cook it for a further 15 minutes.

4 Cook the asparagus in boiling water for 2–3 minutes, drain, and cut into bite-size pieces.

5 Heat the oil in a small skillet and sauté the onion until soft. Spoon the asparagus, onion, and chopped hazelnuts into the prepared pie shell.

6 Beat together the cheese, eggs, and cream until smooth, or process in a blender until smooth.

Season well with salt and pepper, then pour the mixture over the asparagus, onion, and hazelnuts.

7 Bake in the oven for 15–20 minutes, or until the cheese filling is just set. Serve warm or cold.

VARIATION

Omit the hazelnuts and sprinkle Parmesan cheese over the top of the tart just before cooking in the oven, if you prefer.

Onion Tart

Serves 6

INGREDIENTS

9 ounces fresh ready-made
shortcrust pie dough
3 tbsp butter
1/2 cup diced bacon

1 pound 9 ounces onions, peeled
and sliced thinly
2 eggs, beaten
2/3 cup grated Parmesan cheese

1 tsp dried sage
salt and pepper

1 Roll out the pie dough on a lightly floured counter and line a 10-inch loose-bottomed quiche pan.

2 Prick the base of the pie dough all over with a fork and chill for 30 minutes.

3 Heat the butter in a saucepan, add the diced bacon and sliced onions, and sweat them over a low heat for about 25 minutes, or until tender. If the onion slices start to turn brown, add a tablespoon of water to the saucepan.

4 Add the beaten eggs to the onion mixture and stir in the cheese, sage, and salt and pepper to taste. Mix until well combined.

5 Carefully spoon the onion mixture into the prepared pie shell, spreading the mixture to the edges of the shell.

6 Bake in a preheated oven at 350°F for 20–30 minutes, or until the tart has just set.

7 Leave the tart to cool slightly in the pan, then serve the onion tart warm or cold. Cut the tart into slices to serve.

VARIATION

For a vegetarian version, replace the bacon with the same quantity of chopped mushrooms.

Pissaladière

Serves 8

INGREDIENTS

4 tbsp olive oil
1 pound 9 ounces red onions,
thinly sliced
2 garlic cloves, crushed
2 tsp superfine sugar

2 tbsp red wine vinegar
12 ounces fresh ready-made puff
pastry
salt and pepper

TOPPING:
2 1¾ ounce cans anchovy fillets
12 pitted green olives
1 tsp dried marjoram

1 Lightly grease a jelly roll pan with butter. Heat the olive oil in a large saucepan. Add the onions and garlic and cook over a very low heat for about 30 minutes, stirring occasionally, until tender.

2 Add the sugar and vinegar to the pan and season with plenty of salt and pepper to taste. Stir until well combined.

3 On a lightly floured surface, roll out the pastry dough to a rectangle about 13 × 9 inches. Place

the dough rectangle onto the prepared jelly roll pan, pushing the dough well into the corners of the pan.

4 Spread the onion mixture over the dough.

5 Top with the anchovy fillets and green olives, then sprinkle with the marjoram.

6 Bake in a preheated oven at 425°F for about 20–25 minutes, until the pissaladière is a light golden color. Serve piping hot, straight from the oven.

VARIATION

Cut the pissaladière into squares or triangles for easy finger food at a party or barbecue.

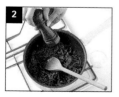

Mini Cheese & Onion Tarts

Serves 12

INGREDIENTS

PIE DOUGH:
1 cup all-purpose flour
¼ tsp salt
⅓ cup butter, cut into small pieces
1–2 tbsp water

FILLING:
1 egg, beaten
generous ⅓ cup light cream
½ cup grated Red Leicester cheese,
3 scallions, finely chopped

salt
cayenne pepper

1 To make the pie dough, sift the flour and salt into a mixing bowl. Rub in the butter with your fingers until well combined and the mixture resembles fine breadcrumbs. Gradually stir in the water, adding little by little, and mix to form a smooth dough.

2 Roll out the pie dough on a lightly floured kitchen surface. Using a 3-inch cookie cutter, stamp out 12 rounds from the dough and line a muffin pan.

3 To make the filling, whisk together the beaten egg, light cream, grated Red Leicester cheese, and chopped scallions. Season with salt and cayenne.

4 Pour the filling mixture into the pie shells and bake in a preheated oven at 350°F for about 20–25 minutes, or until the filling is just set.

5 Serve the mini tarts warm or cold.

VARIATION

Top each mini tart with slices of fresh tomato before baking, if you prefer.

COOK'S TIP

If you use 6 ounces of ready-made pie dough instead of making it yourself, these tarts can be made in minutes.

Ham & Cheese Lattice Pies

Makes 6

INGREDIENTS

9 ounces fresh ready-made puff
pastry
1⅓ cup finely chopped ham

⅔ cup full-fat soft cheese
2 tbsp chopped fresh chives
1 egg, beaten

2 tbsp freshly grated Parmesan
cheese
pepper

1 Roll out the pastry thinly on a lightly floured counter. Cut out 12 rectangles measuring 6 × 2 inches.

2 Place the rectangles onto greased cookie sheets and leave to chill for 30 minutes.

3 Meanwhile, combine the ham, cheese, and chives in a small bowl. Season with pepper to taste.

4 Spread the ham and cheese mixture along the center of 6 of the rectangles, leaving a 1-inch border around each one. Brush the border with a little beaten egg.

5 To make the lattice pattern, fold the remaining rectangles lengthwise. Leaving a 1-inch border, cut vertical lines across one edge of the rectangles using a sharp knife.

6 Unfold the rectangles and place them over the rectangles topped with the ham and cheese mixture set on the cookie sheets. Seal the dough edges well and lightly sprinkle with the grated Parmesan cheese.

7 Bake in a preheated oven at 350°F for 15–20 minutes. Serve hot or cold.

COOK'S TIP

These pies can be made in advance, frozen uncooked, and baked fresh when required.

Curry Turnovers

Serves 4

1¾ cups plain whole-wheat flour
⅓ cup vegan margarine, cut into
    small pieces
4 tbsp water
2 tbsp oil

1¼ cups diced root vegetables
    (potatoes, carrots, and parsnips)
1 small onion, chopped
2 garlic cloves, finely chopped
½ tsp curry powder

½ tsp ground turmeric
½ tsp ground cumin
½ tsp wholegrain mustard
5 tbsp stock
soy milk, to glaze

1 Place the flour in a mixing bowl and rub in the vegan margarine with your fingertips until the mixture resembles breadcrumbs. Stir in the water and bring together to form a soft dough. Wrap and chill in the refrigerator for 30 minutes.

2 To make the filling, heat the oil in a large saucepan. Add the diced root vegetables, chopped onion, and garlic. Sauté for 2 minutes, then stir in all of the spices, turning the vegetables to coat them with the spices. Cook for a further 1 minute.

3 Add the stock to the pan and bring to a boil. Cover and simmer for about 20 minutes, stirring occasionally, until the vegetables are tender and the liquid has been absorbed. Let cool.

4 Divide the pie dough into 4 portions. Roll each portion into a 6-inch round. Place the filling equally on one half of each round.

5 Brush the edges of each round with soy milk, then fold over and press the edges together to seal. Place on a cookie sheet. Bake in a preheated oven at 400°F for 25-30 minutes, until the pastry is a light golden brown color.

Brazil Nut & Mushroom Pie

Serves 4-6

INGREDIENTS

PIE DOUGH:

1¾ cups plain whole-wheat flour
⅓ cup vegan margarine, cut into
    small pieces
4 tbsp water
soy milk, to glaze

FILLING:

2 tbsp vegan margarine
1 onion, chopped
1 garlic clove, finely chopped
2 cups sliced button mushrooms
1 tbsp all-purpose flour
⅔ cup vegetable stock

1 tbsp tomato paste
1½ cups chopped Brazil nuts
1⅓ cups fresh whole-wheat
    breadcrumbs
2 tbsp chopped fresh parsley
½ tsp pepper

1 To make the pie dough, rub the margarine into the flour until it resembles fine breadcrumbs. Stir in the water and bring together to form a dough. Wrap and chill for 30 minutes.

2 Melt the margarine for the filling in a skillet, add the onion, garlic, and mushrooms and sauté for 5 minutes, until softened. Add the flour and cook for 1 minute, stirring. Gradually add the stock, stirring until the sauce is smooth and beginning to thicken. Stir in the tomato paste, Brazil nuts, breadcrumbs, parsley, and pepper. Cool slightly.

3 On a lightly floured surface, roll out two-thirds of the pie dough and use to line an 8-inch loose-bottomed quiche pan or pie dish. Spread the filling in the pie shell. Brush the edges of the pie dough with soy milk. Roll out the remaining pie dough to fit the top of the pie. Seal the edges, make a slit in the top of the pie dough, and brush with soy milk.

4 Bake in a preheated oven at 400°F for 30–40 minutes, until golden brown.

Lentil & Red Bell Pepper Flan

Serves 6-8

INGREDIENTS

PIE DOUGH:

1³/₄ cups plain whole-wheat flour

¹/₃ cup vegan margarine, cut into small pieces

4 tbsp water

FILLING:

³/₄ cup red lentils, rinsed

11/4 cups vegetable stock

1 tbsp vegan margarine

1 onion, chopped

2 red bell peppers, cored, seeded, and diced

1 tsp yeast extract

1 tbsp tomato paste

3 tbsp chopped fresh parsley

pepper

1 To make the pie dough, place the flour in a mixing bowl and rub in the vegan margarine with your fingertips until the mixture resembles fine breadcrumbs. Stir in the water and bring together to form a dough. Wrap and chill in the refrigerator for 30 minutes.

2 Meanwhile, make the filling. Put the lentils in a saucepan with the stock, bring to a boil, and then simmer for 10 minutes, until the lentils are tender and can be mashed to a purée.

3 Melt the margarine in a small pan, add the chopped onion and diced red bell peppers and sauté until just soft.

4 Add the lentil purée, yeast extract, tomato paste, and parsley. Season with pepper. Mix until well combined.

5 On a lightly floured kitchen counter, roll out the dough and line a 10-inch loose-bottomed quiche pan. Prick the base of the pie dough with a fork and spoon the lentil purée mixture into the pie shell.

6 Bake in a preheated oven at 400°F for 30 minutes, until the filling is firm.

Garlic & Sage Bread

Serves 4-6

INGREDIENTS

2¼ cups strong brown bread flour
1 sachet active dry yeast
3 tbsp chopped fresh sage
2 tsp sea salt

3 garlic cloves, finely chopped
1 tsp honey
⅔ cup lukewarm water

1 Grease a cookie sheet. Sift the flour into a large mixing bowl and stir in the husks remaining in the strainer.

2 Stir in the yeast, sage, and half of the sea salt. Reserve 1 teaspoon of the chopped garlic for sprinkling and stir the rest into the bowl. Add the honey with the water and mix together to form a dough.

3 Turn the dough out onto a lightly floured surface and knead it for about 5 minutes

(alternatively, use an electric mixer with a dough hook).

4 Place the dough in a greased bowl, cover, and let rise in a warm place until it has doubled in size.

5 Knead the dough again for a few minutes, shape it into a round and place on the cookie sheet.

6 Cover and let rise for a further 30 minutes, or until springy to the touch. Sprinkle with the rest of the sea salt and garlic.

7 Bake in a preheated oven at 400°F for 25–30 minutes. Cool on a wire rack before serving.

Candies
& Drinks

There is nothing quite as nice as home-made chocolates and candies—they leave the average bought box of chocolates in the shade!

You'll find recipes in this chapter to suit everybody's taste. Wonderful, rich, melt-in-the-mouth chocolate truffles, crispy florentines, nutty chocolate creams, and rich chocolate liqueurs—they're all here. There is even some simple-to-make chocolate fudge, so there is no need to fiddle about with sugar thermometers.

Looking for something to wash it all down? We have included two delightfully cool summer chocolate drinks, and for warmth and comfort on winter nights, two hot drinks that will simply put instant hot chocolate to shame. Enjoy!

Rocky Road Bites

Makes 18

INGREDIENTS

4¹/₂ ounces milk chocolate
2¹/₂ ounces mini multicolored
  marshmallows

¹/₄ cup chopped walnuts
1 ounce no-need-to-soak dried
  apricots, chopped

1 Line a cookie sheet with baking parchment and set aside.

2 Break the milk chocolate into small pieces and melt in a double boiler.

3 Stir in the marshmallows, walnuts, and apricots and toss in the melted chocolate until the ingredients are completely coated in the chocolate.

4 Place heaping teaspoons of the mixture onto the prepared cookie sheet.

5 Chill the candies in the refrigerator until they are completely set.

6 Once set, carefully remove the candies from the baking parchment.

7 The chewy bites can be placed in paper candy cases to serve, if desired.

COOK'S TIP

These candies can be stored in a cool, dry place for up to 2 weeks.

VARIATION

Light, fluffy marshmallows are available in white or pastel colors. If you cannot find mini marshmallows, use large ones and snip them into smaller pieces with kitchen scissors before mixing them into the melted chocolate in step 3.

Easy Chocolate Fudge

Makes 25–30 pieces

INGREDIENTS

1 lb 2 ounces dark chocolate	14 ounce can sweetened condensed	½ tsp vanilla extract
⅓ cup sweet butter	milk	

1 Lightly grease an 8-inch square cake pan.

2 Break the chocolate into pieces and place in a large saucepan with the butter and condensed milk.

3 Heat gently, stirring until the chocolate and butter melt and the mixture is smooth. Do not allow to boil.

4 Remove the pan from the heat. Beat in the vanilla extract, then beat the mixture for a few minutes until thickened. Pour it into the prepared pan and level the top.

5 Chill the mixture in the refrigerator until firm.

6 Tip the fudge out onto a cutting board and cut into squares to serve.

VARIATION

For chocolate peanut fudge, replace 4 tablespoons of the butter with crunchy peanut butter.

COOK'S TIP

Store the fudge in an airtight container in a cool, dry place for up to 1 month. Do not freeze.

COOK'S TIP

Don't use milk chocolate as the results will be too sticky.

No-Cook Fruit & Nut Chocolate Fudge

Makes about 25 pieces

INGREDIENTS

9 ounces dark chocolate
2 tbsp butter

4 tbsp evaporated milk
3 cups confectioners' sugar, sifted

½ cup roughly chopped hazelnuts
⅓ cup golden raisins

1 Lightly grease an 8-inch square cake pan.

2 Break the chocolate into pieces and melt in a double boiler with the butter and evaporated milk. Stir until the chocolate and butter have melted and the ingredients are well combined.

3 Remove from the heat and gradually beat in the confectioners' sugar. Stir the hazelnuts and golden raisins into the mixture. Press the fudge into the prepared pan and level the top. Chill until firm.

4 Tip the fudge out onto a cutting board and cut into squares. Place in paper candy cases. Chill until required.

VARIATION

Vary the nuts used in this recipe; try making the fudge with almonds, brazil nuts, walnuts, or pecans.

COOK'S TIP

The fudge can be stored in an airtight container for up to 2 weeks.

Nutty Chocolate Clusters

Makes about 30

INGREDIENTS

6 ounces white chocolate
3½ ounces graham crackers

1 cup chopped macadamia nuts or
brazil nuts

1 ounce preserved ginger,
chopped (optional)
6 ounces dark chocolate

1 Line a cookie sheet with baking parchment. Break the white chocolate into small pieces and melt in a double boiler.

2 Break the graham crackers into small pieces. Stir the graham crackers into the melted chocolate, together with the chopped nuts and preserved ginger, if using.

3 Place heaping teaspoons of the mixture onto the prepared cookie sheet.

4 Chill the mixture in the refrigerator until set, then carefully remove the clusters from the baking parchment.

5 Melt the dark chocolate and let cool slightly. Dip the clusters into the melted chocolate, allowing the excess to drip back into the bowl. Return the clusters to the cookie sheet and chill in the refrigerator until set.

COOK'S TIP

The clusters can be stored for up to 1 week in a cool, dry place.

COOK'S TIP

Macadamia and brazil nuts are both rich-tasting and high in fat, which makes them particularly popular for confectionery, but other nuts can be used, if desired.

Chocolate Cherries

Makes 24

INGREDIENTS

12 candied cherries
2 tbsp rum or brandy

9 ounces marzipan
5½ ounces dark chocolate

extra milk, dark, or white chocolate,
to decorate (optional)

1 Line a cookie sheet with baking parchment.

2 Cut the cherries in half and place them in a small bowl. Add the rum or brandy and stir to coat. Set the cherries aside to soak for a minimum of 1 hour, stirring occasionally.

3 Divide the marzipan into 24 pieces and roll each piece into a ball. Press half a marinated cherry into the top of each marzipan ball.

4 Break the chocolate into pieces and melt in a double boiler.

5 Dip each candy into the melted chocolate, allowing the excess to drip back into the pan. Place the coated cherries on the baking parchment and chill until set.

6 If desired, melt a little extra chocolate and drizzle it over the top of the coated cherries. Let set.

VARIATION

Flatten the marzipan and use it to mold around the cherries to cover them, then dip in the chocolate as above.

VARIATION

Use a whole almond in place of the halved candied cherries and omit the rum or brandy.

484

Chocolate Marzipans

Makes about 30

INGREDIENTS

1 pound marzipan
⅓ cup very finely chopped
   candied cherries

1 ounce preserved ginger, very
   finely chopped
¼ cup no-need-to-soak dried
   apricots, very finely chopped

12 ounces dark chocolate
1 ounces white chocolate
confectioners' sugar, to dust

1   Line a cookie sheet with baking parchment. Divide the marzipan into 3 balls and knead each ball to soften it.

2   Work the candied cherries into one portion of the marzipan by kneading on a surface lightly dusted with confectioners' sugar.

3   Work the preserved ginger into a second portion of marzipan, and then work the apricots into the third portion of marzipan in the same way.

4   Form each flavored portion of marzipan into small balls, making sure the flavors are kept separate.

5   Melt the dark chocolate in a double boiler. Dip one of each flavored ball of marzipan into the chocolate by spiking each one with a toothpick, allowing the excess chocolate to drip back into the pan.

6   Carefully place the balls in clusters of the three flavors on the prepared cookie sheet. Repeat with

the remaining marzipan balls. Chill until set.

7   Melt the white chocolate and drizzle a little over the tops of each cluster of marzipan balls. Chill until hardened, then remove from the baking parchment and dust with sugar to serve.

VARIATION

Coat the marzipan balls in white or milk chocolate and drizzle with dark chocolate, if desired.

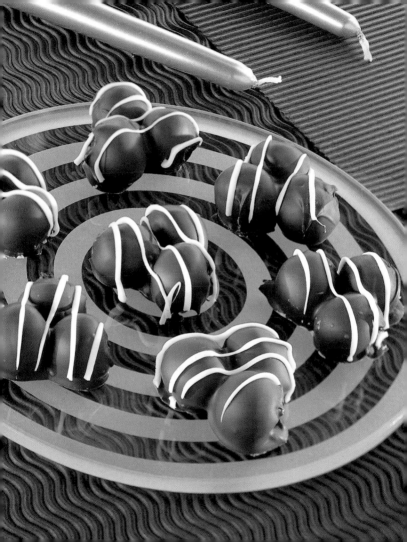

Chocolate Liqueurs

Makes 20

INGREDIENTS

3¹/₂ ounces dark chocolate

about 5 candied cherries, halved

about 10 hazelnuts or

    macadamia nuts

²/₃ cup heavy cream

2 tbsp confectioners' sugar

4 tbsp liqueur

TO FINISH:

1³/₄ ounces dark chocolate, melted

a little white chocolate, melted,

    or white chocolate curls

    or extra nuts and cherries

1 Line a cookie sheet with baking parchment. Melt the chocolate and spoon it into 20 paper candy cases, spreading up the sides with a small spoon or pastry brush. Place upside down on the prepared cookie sheet and let set.

2 Carefully peel away the paper cases. Place a cherry or nut in the base of each cup.

3 To make the filling, place the heavy cream in a mixing bowl and sift the confectioners' sugar on top. Whip the cream until it is just holding its shape, then beat in the liqueur.

4 Place the cream in a pastry bag fitted with a ¹/₂-inch plain tip and pipe a little into each chocolate case. Set aside in the refrigerator to chill for 20 minutes.

5 To finish, spoon the melted dark chocolate over the cream to cover it, and pipe the melted white chocolate on top, swirling it into the dark chocolate with a toothpick. Set aside to harden. Alternatively, cover the cream with the melted dark chocolate and decorate with white chocolate curls before setting. Or, place a small piece of nut or cherry on top of the cream and then cover with dark chocolate.

COOK'S TIP

Candy cases can vary in size. Use the smallest you can find for this recipe.

Chocolate Cups with Mascarpone Filling

Makes 20

INGREDIENTS

3½ ounces dark chocolate

FILLING:
3½ ounces milk or dark chocolate
¼ tsp vanilla extract

1 cup mascarpone cheese
unsweetened cocoa, to dust

1 Line a cookie sheet with baking parchment. Melt the chocolate and spoon it into 20 paper candy cases, spreading up the sides with a small spoon or pastry brush. Place upside down on the prepared cookie sheet and let set.

2 When set, carefully peel away the paper cases.

3 To make the filling, melt the dark or milk chocolate. Place the mascarpone cheese in a bowl, beat in the vanilla extract and melted chocolate, and beat until well combined. Chill the mixture in the refrigerator, beating occasionally until firm enough to pipe.

4 Place the mascarpone filling in a pastry bag fitted with a star tip and pipe the mixture into the cups. Decorate with a dusting of unsweetened cocoa.

COOK'S TIP

Mascarpone is a rich Italian soft cheese made from fresh cream, so it has a high fat content. Its delicate flavor blends well with chocolate.

VARIATION

You can use lightly whipped heavy cream instead of the mascarpone cheese, if desired.

Mini Chocolate Cones

Makes 10

INGREDIENTS

2³/₄ ounces dark chocolate
¹/₃ cup heavy cream

1 tbsp confectioners' sugar
1 tbsp crème de menthe

chocolate coffee beans, to
decorate (optional)

1 Cut ten 3-inch rounds of baking parchment. Shape each round into a cone shape and secure with tape.

2 Melt the chocolate. Using a small pastry brush or clean artists' brush, brush the inside of each cone with melted chocolate.

3 Brush a second layer of chocolate on the inside of the cones and chill until set. Carefully peel away the paper.

4 Place the heavy cream, confectioners' sugar, and crème de menthe in a mixing bowl and whip until just holding its shape. Place in a pastry bag fitted with a star tip and pipe the mixture into the chocolate cones.

5 Decorate the cones with chocolate coffee beans (if using) and chill in the refrigerator until required.

COOK'S TIP

The chocolate cones can be made in advance and kept in the refrigerator for up to 1 week. Do not fill them more than 2 hours before you are going to serve them.

VARIATION

Use a different flavored liqueur to flavor the cream: a coffee-flavored liqueur is perfect. If you want a mint flavor without using a liqueur, use a few drops of peppermint extract to flavor the cream, according to taste.

Collettes

Makes 20

INGREDIENTS

3 1/2 ounces white chocolate

FILLING:
5 1/2 ounces orange-flavored
dark chocolate

2/3 cup heavy cream
2 tbsp confectioners' sugar

1 Line a cookie sheet with baking parchment. Melt the chocolate and spoon it into 20 paper candy cases, spreading up the sides with a small spoon or pastry brush. Place upside down on the prepared cookie sheet and let set.

2 When set, carefully peel away the paper cases.

3 To make the filling, melt the orange-flavored chocolate and place in a mixing bowl with the heavy cream and the confectioners' sugar. Beat until smooth.

Chill in the refrigerator, stirring occasionally, until the mixture becomes firm enough to pipe.

4 Place the filling in a pastry bag fitted with a star tip and pipe a little into each case. Chill in the refrigerator until required.

VARIATION

Add 1 tbsp orange-flavored liqueur to the filling, if desired.

COOK'S TIP

If they do not hold their shape well, use 2 cases to make a double thickness mold. Foil cases are firmer, so use these if desired.

Use the smallest candy cases you can find for these cups.

Mini Florentines

Makes about 40

INGREDIENTS

⅓ cup butter	2 tbsp chopped candied cherries	¾ cup slivered almonds
⅓ cup superfine sugar	2 tbsp candied ginger, chopped	2 tbsp heavy cream
2 tbsp golden raisins	¼ cup sunflower seeds	6 ounces dark or milk chocolate

1 Lightly grease and flour 2 cookie sheets or line with baking parchment. Place the butter in a small pan and heat gently until melted. Add the sugar, stir until dissolved, then bring the mixture to a boil. Remove from the heat and stir in the golden raisins, cherries, ginger, sunflower seeds, and almonds. Mix well, then beat in the cream.

2 Place small teaspoons of the fruit and nut mixture onto the prepared cookie sheets, allowing plenty of space for the mixture to spread. Bake in a preheated oven at 350°F for 10–12 minutes, until light golden in color.

3 Remove from the oven and, while still hot, use a circular cookie cutter to pull in the edges to form a perfect round. Let cool and crispen before removing from the cookie sheet.

4 Melt most of the chocolate and spread it on a sheet of baking parchment. When the chocolate is on the point of setting, place the cookies, flat side down, on the chocolate and allow to harden completely.

5 Cut around the florentines and remove from the paper. Spread a little more chocolate on the already coated side of the florentines and use a fork to mark waves in the chocolate. Let set. Arrange the florentines on a plate (or in a presentation box for a gift), with alternate sides facing upward. Keep cool.

Mini Chocolate Tartlets

Makes about 18

INGREDIENTS

1½ cups all-purpose flour
⅓ cup butter
1 tbsp superfine sugar
about 1 tbsp water

FILLING:
½ cup cream cheese
5 tsp superfine sugar
1 small egg, lightly beaten
1¾ ounces dark chocolate

TO DECORATE:
⅓ cup heavy cream
dark chocolate curls
unsweetened cocoa, to dust

1 Sift the flour into a mixing bowl. Cut the butter into small pieces and rub it in with your fingertips until the mixture resembles fine breadcrumbs. Stir in the sugar. Add just enough water to mix to a soft dough, then cover, and chill in the refrigerator for 15 minutes.

2 Roll out the pie dough on a lightly floured surface and use to line 18 mini tartlet pans or mini muffin pans. Prick the bases with a toothpick.

3 Beat together the cream cheese and the sugar until smooth. Beat in the egg. Melt the chocolate and beat it into the mixture. Spoon into the pie shells and bake in a preheated oven at 375°F for about 15 minutes, until the pastry is crisp and the filling set. Place the pans on a wire rack to cool completely.

4 Chill the tartlets in the refrigerator. Whip the cream until it is just holding its shape. Place in a pastry bag fitted with a star tip. Pipe rosettes of cream on top of the tartlets. Decorate with chocolate curls and dust with unsweetened cocoa.

COOK'S TIP

The tartlets can be made up to 3 days ahead. Decorate on the day of serving, preferably no more than 4 hours in advance.

Rum Truffles

Makes about 20

INGREDIENTS

5¹/₂ ounces dark chocolate
small pat of butter
2 tbsp rum

¹/₂ cup shredded coconut
2 cups cake crumbs

6 tbsp confectioners' sugar
2 tbsp unsweetened cocoa

1 Break the chocolate into pieces and melt with the butter in a double boiler.

2 Remove the melted chocolate from the heat and beat in the rum. Stir in the shredded coconut, cake crumbs, and 4 tablespoons of the confectioners' sugar. Beat until well combined. Add a little extra rum if the mixture is too stiff.

3 Roll the mixture into small, evenly-sized balls and place them on a sheet of baking parchment. Chill in the refrigerator until firm.

4 Sift the remaining confectioners' sugar onto a large plate. Sift the unsweetened cocoa onto another plate. Roll half of the truffles in the confectioners' sugar until coated, and roll the remaining truffles in the unsweetened cocoa.

5 Place the truffles in paper candy cases and chill in the refrigerator until required.

VARIATION

Make the truffles with white chocolate and replace the rum with coconut liqueur. Roll them in unsweetened cocoa or dip in melted milk chocolate.

COOK'S TIP

These truffles will keep for about 2 weeks in a cool place.

White Chocolate Truffles

Makes about 20

INGREDIENTS

2 tbsp sweet butter

5 tbsp heavy cream

8 ounces good quality Swiss
white chocolate

1 tbsp orange-flavored liqueur
(optional)

TO FINISH:

3½ ounces white chocolate

1 Line a jelly roll pan with baking parchment.

2 Place the butter and cream in a small saucepan and bring slowly to a boil, stirring constantly. Boil for 1 minute, then remove from the heat.

3 Break the chocolate into pieces and add to the cream. Stir until melted, then beat in the liqueur, if using.

4 Pour into the prepared pan and chill for about 2 hours until firm.

5 Break off pieces of mixture and roll them into balls. Chill for a further 30 minutes before finishing the truffles.

6 To finish, melt the white chocolate. Dip the balls in the chocolate, allowing the excess to drip back into the bowl. Place on nonstick baking parchment and swirl the chocolate with a fork. Let harden.

7 Drizzle a little melted dark chocolate over the truffles if desired and let set. Place the truffles in paper cases to serve.

COOK'S TIP

The truffle mixture needs to be firm, but not too hard to roll. If the mixture is too hard, allow it to stand at room temperature for a few minutes to soften slightly. During rolling the mixture will become sticky but will re-harden in the refrigerator before coating.

COOK'S TIP

The chocolates can be kept in the refrigerator for up to 2 weeks.

Italian Chocolate Truffles

Makes about 24

INGREDIENTS

6 ounces dark chocolate
2 tbsp almond-flavored
   liqueur (amaretto) or orange-
   flavored liqueur

3 tbsp sweet butter
1/2 cup confectioners' sugar

1/2 cup ground almonds
1 3/4 ounces grated chocolate

1 Melt the dark chocolate with the liqueur in a double boiler, stirring until well combined.

2 Add the butter and stir until it has melted. Stir in the confectioners' sugar and the ground almonds.

3 Leave the mixture in a cool place until firm enough to roll into about 24 balls.

4 Place the grated chocolate on a plate and roll the truffles in the chocolate to coat them.

5 Place the truffles in paper candy cases and chill.

COOK'S TIP

These truffles will keep for about 2 weeks in a cool place.

VARIATION

The almond-flavored liqueur gives these truffles an authentic Italian flavor. The original almond liqueur, Amaretto di Saronno, comes from Saronno in Italy.

VARIATION

For a sweeter truffle, use milk chocolate instead of dark. Dip the truffles in melted chocolate to finish, if desired.

Hot Chocolate Drinks

Serves 2

INGREDIENTS

SPICY HOT CHOCOLATE:
2¹/₂ cups milk
1 tsp apple pie spice
3¹/₂ ounces dark chocolate
4 cinnamon sticks

¹/₃ cup heavy cream, lightly
  whipped

HOT CHOCOLATE & ORANGE TODDY:
2¹/₂ ounces orange-flavored
  dark chocolate

2¹/₂ cups milk
3 tbsp rum
2 tbsp heavy cream
grated nutmeg

1 To make Spicy Hot Chocolate, pour the milk into a small pan. Sprinkle the apple pie spice into the pan.

2 Break the dark chocolate into squares and add to the milk. Heat the mixture over a low heat until the milk is just boiling, stirring all the time to prevent the milk from burning on the bottom of the pan.

3 Place 2 cinnamon sticks in 2 cups and pour in the spicy hot chocolate. Top with the whipped heavy cream and serve immediately.

4 To make Hot Chocolate & Orange Toddy, break the orange-flavored dark chocolate into squares and place in a small saucepan with the milk. Heat over a low heat until just boiling, stirring constantly.

5 Remove the pan the heat and stir in the rum. Pour into cups.

6 Pour the cream over the back of a spoon or swirl onto the top so that it sits on top of the hot chocolate. Sprinkle with grated nutmeg and serve at once.

COOK'S TIP

Using a cinnamon stick as a stirrer will give any hot chocolate drink a sweet, pungent flavor of cinnamon, without overpowering the flavor of the chocolate.

Cold Chocolate Drinks

Serves 2

INGREDIENTS

CHOCOLATE MILK SHAKE:

2 cups ice-cold milk

3 tbsp drinking chocolate powder

3 scoops chocolate ice cream

unsweetened cocoa powder, to dust
(optional)

CHOCOLATE ICE CREAM SODA:

5 tbsp chocolate dessert sauce

soda water

2 scoops chocolate ice cream

heavy cream, whipped

dark or milk chocolate, grated

1 To make Chocolate Milk Shake, place half the ice-cold milk in a blender.

2 Add the chocolate powder to the blender and 1 scoop of the chocolate ice cream. Blend until the mixture is frothy and well mixed. Stir in the remaining milk.

3 Place the remaining 2 scoops of chocolate ice cream in 2 serving glasses and carefully pour the chocolate milk over the ice cream.

4 Sprinkle a little unsweetened cocoa (if using) over the top of each drink and serve at once.

5 To make Chocolate Ice Cream Soda, divide the chocolate dessert sauce between 2 glasses.

6 Add a little soda water to each glass and stir to combine the sauce and soda water. Place a scoop of ice cream in each glass and top up with more soda water.

7 Place a large spoon of whipped cream on the top, if desired, and sprinkle with a little grated dark or milk chocolate.

COOK'S TIP

Served in a tall glass, a milk shake or an ice cream soda makes a scrumptious snack in a drink. Serve with straws, if wished.

Index